# WALKING THE CAMIÑO DOS FAROS

## About the Author

John Hayes is a retired management consultant with degrees from Liverpool University and University College London. Immediately after finishing work in 2011 he embarked on an epic 5000km trek across Europe, walking from Tarifa in Spain to Budapest. John has written for numerous walking and trekking magazines.

The *Camiño dos Faros* is John's fourth guide for Cicerone. His first cycling guide – *the Ruta Vía de la Plata* – is scheduled for publication in 2020. www.johnhayeswalks.com

**Other Cicerone guides by the author**

*The GR1: Spain's Sendero Histórico*

*Trekking Munich to Venice: The Traumpfad, 'Dream Way', a classic trek across the eastern Alps*

*The Karnischer Höhenweg: The Carnic Peace Trail: Austria and Italy*

# WALKING THE CAMIÑO DOS FAROS

## THE WAY OF THE LIGHTHOUSES ON SPAIN'S GALICIAN COAST

by John Hayes

CICERONE

JUNIPER HOUSE, MURLEY MOSS,
OXENHOLME ROAD, KENDAL, CUMBRIA LA9 7RL
www.cicerone.co.uk

First edition 2019
ISBN: 978 1 85284 971 9

Printed in China on behalf of Latitude Press Ltd
A catalogue record for this book is available from the British Library.

Route mapping by Lovell Johns www.lovelljohns.com
All photographs are by the author unless otherwise stated.



**Updates to this Guide**

While every effort is made by our authors to ensure the accuracy of guidebooks as they go to print, changes can occur during the lifetime of an edition. Any updates that we know of for this guide will be on the Cicerone website (www.cicerone.co.uk/971/updates), so please check before planning your trip. We also advise that you check information about such things as transport, accommodation and shops locally. Even rights of way can be altered over time.

The route maps in this guide are derived from publicly available data, databases and crowd-sourced data. As such they have not been through the detailed checking procedures that would generally be applied to a published map from an official mapping agency, although naturally we have reviewed them closely in the light of local knowledge as part of the preparation of this guide.

We are always grateful for information about any discrepancies between a guidebook and the facts on the ground, sent by email to updates@cicerone.co.uk or by post to Cicerone, Juniper House, Murley Moss, Oxenholme Road, Kendal, LA9 7RL.

**Register your book:** To sign up to receive free updates, special offers and GPX files where available, register your book at www.cicerone.co.uk.

*Front cover:* Looking back to Laxe on Stage 4

# CONTENTS

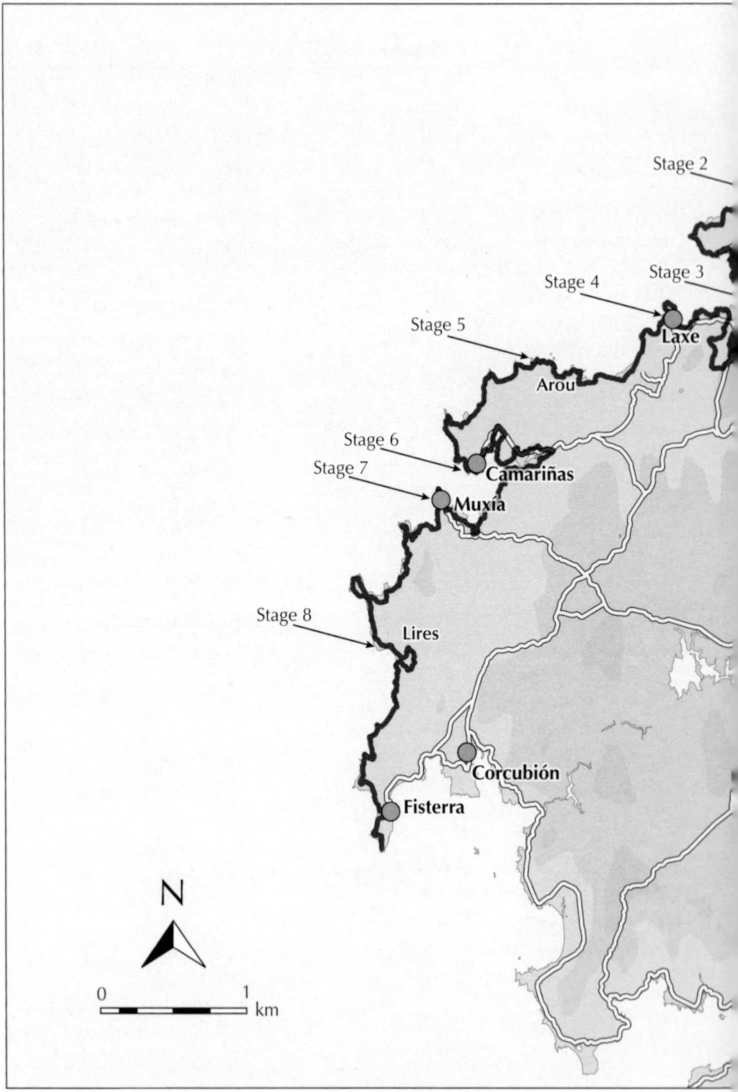
Stage 2
Stage 3
Stage 4
Laxe
Stage 5
Arou
Stage 6
Camariñas
Stage 7
Muxía
Stage 8
Lires
Corcubión
Fisterra
N
0
1
km

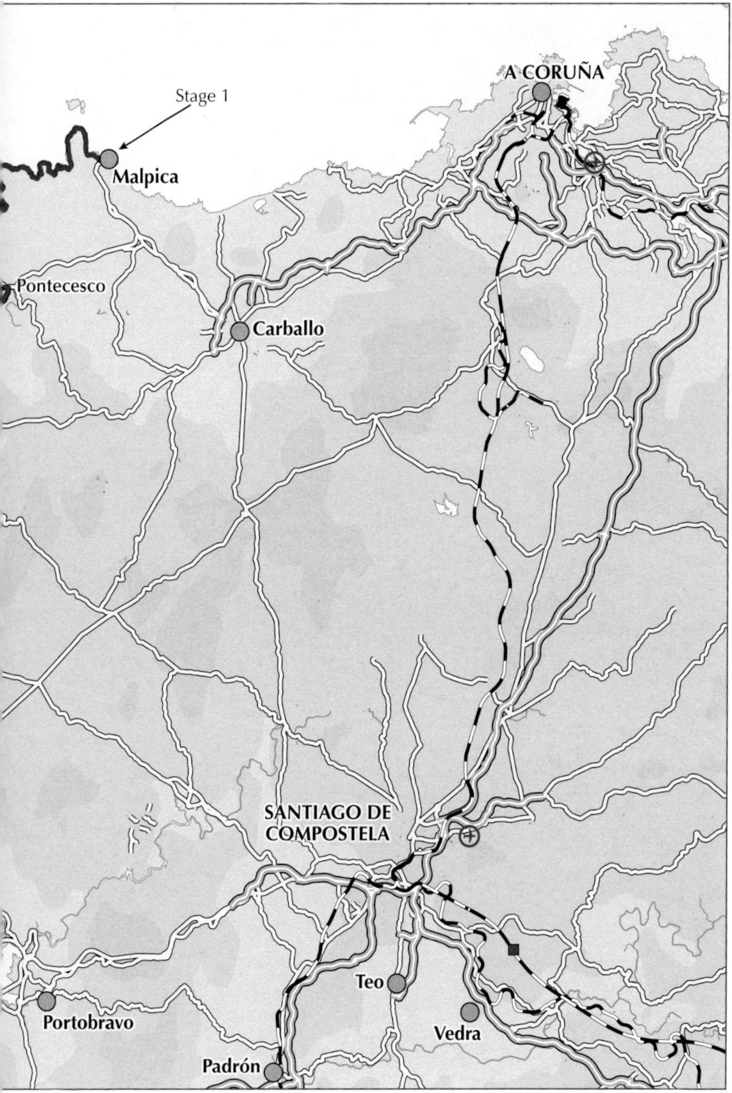
A CORUÑA
Stage 1
Malpica
Pontecesco
Carballo
SANTIAGO DE COMPOSTELA
Teo
Portobravo
Vedra
Padrón

## Symbols used on route maps

| | |
|---|---|
| route | start point |
| alternative route | finish point |
| woodland | peak |
| urban areas | manned/unmanned refuge |
| regional border | parking |
| international border | church/monastery/cross |
| station/railway | lighthouse |
| wind turbines | |

SCALE: 1:50,000

0 kilometres 0.5 1

0 miles 0.5

Contour lines are drawn at 25m intervals and highlighted at 100m intervals.

**Relief**
in metres

600–800
400–600
200–400
0–200

**GPX files** for all routes can be downloaded free at www.cicerone.co.uk/971/GPX.

*Looking back to Petón do Castro (Stage 4)*

# ROUTE SUMMARY TABLE

| Stage | Start | Finish | Distance | Ascent | Time | Page |
|---|---|---|---|---|---|---|
| 1 | Malpica | Praia de Niñóns | 22km | 740m | 6hr | 28 |
| 2 | Praia de Niñóns | Ponteceso | 26km | 510m | 7hr 45min | 38 |
| 3 | Ponteceso | Laxe | 25km | 430m | 6hr 35min | 48 |
| 4 | Laxe | Arou | 18km | 210m | 6hr | 58 |
| 5 | Arou | Camariñas | 23km | 300m | 7hr 40min | 65 |
| 6 | Camariñas | Muxía | 29.5km | 470m | 8hr 40min | 75 |
| 7 | Muxía | Praia de Nemiña | 26.5km | 910m | 7hr 25min | 84 |
| 8 | Praia de Nemiña | Cabo Fisterra | 27km | 820m | 7hr 50min | 93 |
| Total | | | 197km | 4390m | 57hr 55min | |

Faro de Punta Nariga (Stage 1)

# INTRODUCTION

The Camiño dos Faros, the Way of the Lighthouses, follows one of the most beautiful and interesting stretches of coastline in Europe. Located in the northwest corner of Spain it visits the cliffs, bays and beaches of the Costa da Morte.

The Camiño dos Faros is a newly established route. It was the vision of six childhood friends, lovers of all things Galician, who set themselves a simple challenge – to create a trail that goes as close to the sea as possible from Malpica to Fisterra. The vision has now been delivered and the route is enjoyed by hundreds of walkers who each year complete one of more of its eight stages.

The Camiño dos Faros visits a series of lighthouses – lighthouses sited to help sailors navigate one of the world's most dangerous stretches of water. The stretch of coast between Malpica and Fisterra is known as the Costa da Morte, the coast of death. It's a name probably given to the coast by British sailors, many of whom lost their lives on its rocks and reefs.

The journey around Spain's northwest corner takes time. Changing direction from west to south is only achieved after navigating several peninsulas, bays and estuaries. This makes for a walk of great variety, whose mood changes constantly. Within the space of an hour, it can take you from an exposed cliff top – windy and wild, with huge views out to sea – down to a sandy river estuary, which is quiet, sheltered and intimate.

The Camiño dos Faros starts in Malpica, a cosy ex-whaling port on the northern coast. It finishes at Fisterra, Spain's Land's End. It is just under 200km long and is designed to be completed in eight days. Six of the eight days involve a mix of cliff tops and beaches while two days take you around large rias along what is a very indented coastline.

The walking is not technically difficult, but like many coastal walks it can be hard work. Although there are no big ascents, there are a lot of small ones: sticking rigorously to the coastline doesn't usually mean taking fastest route between A and B. Completing the whole of the Camiño dos Faros in eight days is fairly challenging, but fortunately there are ways to make it easier. There is enough to see and experience to justify a longer trip if time is available.

The six childhood friends who created the Camiño dos Faros are a group of modest individuals who keep their identity almost invisible. What has been achieved however since they first walked the route in 2012 has been immense. They plotted a route, waymarked it, developed an excellent website (www.caminodosfaros.com), maintain a lively Facebook page, and manage an annual walk programme with each event involving the participation of many hundreds of people. They have an organisation to manage the development of the route, Association O Camiño dos Faros. The walk has its own branding and this is reflected in a range of merchandise sold in Malpica at the Association clubhouse and shop. The importance of route is widely recognised and well supported by local hoteliers, restaurateurs and taxi drivers. In addition to the original trail there is now also a mountain bike route, an annual run and even a group of hardy individuals who are attempting to complete the 'route' by kayak. The term 'tranos', used to describe the original group, is now applied to anyone who travels along the Camiño dos Faros.

Walking a trail invented and supported by the local community gives a particular flavour to the experience. Sustaining the route, however, through wild remote countryside – much of which has now been abandoned by agriculture – is a major challenge. Galicia has a mild, wet climate and things grow quickly. Fortunately, and thanks in large part to the work of the Association, the importance of the route has now been recognised by all levels of government and funding has been obtained to ensure the path is clear enough to be hiked. The route is in the process of conversion to a Gran Recorrido (GR), and funding has been secured to waymark it with the route using the white and red symbol used across Spain and much of Europe.

The Association has welcomed the development of this guide and have been incredibly generous with their ideas and time, which have been much appreciated.

*Faro do Cabo Vilán (Stage 5)*

Castro a Cibdá de Borneiro (Stage 3)

## CAMIÑO DOS FAROS – A GALICIAN COASTAL WALK

If you're lucky enough to walk some of the route with a local then it soon becomes clear that the Camiño dos Faros is, in part at least, a celebration of Galicia and its way of life.

Spain is a country famously made up of regions, some of which are fiercely loyal to their own culture and identity. Galicia has that same sense of identity, although the extent to which it is expressed politically is more muted than in Catalonia and the Basque Country. Galicia has its own language, Galego, and a distinct culture, featuring ancient myths and traditions which are celebrated and kept alive.

Galician's regard themselves as Celtic and see other Atlantic communities in Brittany, Cornwall, Wales, Scotland and Ireland, as their brethren. While evidence for a 'Celtic family' is controversial (Galego is not a Gaelic language and has a stronger affinity to Portuguese), the sentiment is real enough and communities around the northwest Atlantic share some common features. As well as having similar climates and geology all are (or were) positioned at the edge of countries run from large, sometimes unresponsive, metropolitan centres. They have all suffered economically as a result of their remote location and lost population through migration (some say that Buenos Aires is the largest Galician city). A common response has been to focus on their own resources, discover what makes them special, and celebrate it.

Language is important. Galego, overshadowed for centuries by Castilian Spanish, was once the language of troubadours and used in songs of love, life and death across the Iberian peninsula. Like other threatened Atlantic community languages

it went through a huge revival in the 19th century and, led by Galician romantic writers like Rosalía de Castro and Eduardo Pondal, was reinvented as a literary, written language. Now, two-thirds of Galicians have grown up with it as the main or shared language of their household; this is much higher than the proportion of Euskara-speaking Basque people or Catalan-speaking Catalonians.

Location is also important. Positioned where the sun sets into the Atlantic, where people historically thought the earth ended and the afterlife started, this is a place rich in legend and myth. Included in a long list of supernatural creatures are *meigas* and *brujas* (good and bad witches), *mouros* (huge beasts who hoard treasure under abandoned iron age settlements or *castro*), *nereidas* (evil seductive fish women), and *mouchas*, (owl-like spirits whose calls announce death's arrival). There are also werewolves, the *lobishomes*, although their significance may be due to the fact that real wolves – never completely wiped out in northwest Spain – still roam the local countryside.

Like other Atlantic communities, the Galicians gave the Romans a hard time and evidence of a particularly strong pre-Roman community is still abundant. In particular, there are some 5000 *castros*. One of the most important, the Castro a Cibdá de Borneiro, is on the route, as is

*Approaching the Punta da Castelo (Stage 8)*

an example of an even older burial chamber, the Dólmen de Dombate.

Pre-Roman, pre-Christian and Christian traditions blend in a particularly Galician way in the dense annual calendar of fiestas in the villages and towns along the Camiño dos Faros. A schedule of the most important ones is included in this book (Appendix C) and it's worth planning a trip with a least one of the dates in mind. Based on a sample of one (the July Festa da Virxe do Carme in Camariñas), what was striking were the costumes and the dancing which, to an untutored eye, were very reminiscent of English morris dancers; also noticeable were the bagpipes, a very Celtic instrument.

## CAMIÑO DOS FAROS AND THE SEA

It's stating the obvious to point out that a route that goes from lighthouse to lighthouse features the sea and embracing the fact greatly enhances the enjoyment of the trip. This is coastal walk that visits a series of communities that make their living from seafood. The Spanish love fish, the best fish comes from Galicia, and Galicians are experts in all things to do with fish: catching them; growing them; harvesting them; processing them; and, of course, eating them.

Galician fisherman, sometimes controversially, travel far and wide to satisfy the Spanish demand for fish and the little ports along the Costa da

Morte feature modern trawlers and ice plants. It's still a dangerous occupation and, on average, some 20 fishermen lose their lives annually – that's around 80% of the Spanish total.

The entire Galician coastline is known as the Costa do Marisco and shellfish are as important to the local economy as deepwater fish. Many of the shellfish consumed will be familiar (although few communities elsewhere consume them with the same gusto). These include *ameixas* (clams), *cigala* (langoustines/scampi), *gamba* (shrimp), *mexillóus* (mussels) and *vieras* (scallops). Others are a little more esoteric, including; *nécora* (velvet crab), *centolo* (spider crab), and *navallas* (razor clams). Some are positively exotic, in particular the *percebes*. Percebes, or gooseneck barnacles, grow on rocks at the point where the waves break and harvesting them is a heroic activity involving men in wetsuits, anchored by ropes to the rocks above, scrambling around in the surf with a bucket.

If like me, you're from the UK where most of the fish consumed are cod or haddock deep fried in batter, eating seafood in Galicia can be intimidating; a little bravery however brings great rewards. My personal favourites are the razor clams and percebes consumed of course with a local Galician white wine, either an Albariño or a Godello.

The fishing industry in Galicia is currently doing well, but historically it's been a tough way to make a living in what is a poor part of Spain. The decline of fish stocks and the closure of traditional fishing grounds, the price of oil, and wider problems in the Spanish economy ushered in hard times. The fluctuating economy partly explains why a less savoury relationship with the sea emerged to compensate: drug smuggling. Galicia is apparently Europe's number one coastline for the entry of hard drugs, including cocaine from Columbia. Inevitably this has resulted in a thriving underworld with links to other cartels around Europe including the UK.

## THE COSTA DA MORTE

For ships heading to and from northern Europe to the Mediterranean, and beyond, staying reasonably close to the coast as they round the northwest corner of Spain is the most direct route; it's also very dangerous.

The history of the Costa da Morte is particularly interesting from a British perspective and in many ways tracks both the rise and decline of the British Empire. In the competition for global naval dominance, the coast just off Fisterra has seen many key events. The second Spanish Armada came to grief here, and the British Navy won crucial victories over France/Spain in the Spanish Wars of Succession and the Napoleonic Wars. British-built ships – first sail, then steam, and part of the world's biggest merchant marine – carried the lion's share of 19th century global trade and it was these ships, often loaded with coal, which came to grief on the reefs and rocks of the Costa da Morte. Some of the most important British Navy safety innovations, for instance the use of life jackets throughout the British Navy, were made as a result of disasters along this stretch of coast. The term 'Costa da Morte' had become common parlance among British seafarers by the 19th century.

The lighthouses themselves are the most tangible reminder that this is a coastline where small navigational errors can have catastrophic consequences. Developed progressively during the 19th century, the biggest and most impressive lighthouse – the Faro Vilán – was built in 1895, and followed a particularly dreadful series of disasters where shipwrecks were occurring on an annual basis.

The lighthouses, impressive as they are, have not rendered the Costa da Morte safe and shipwrecks continue to happen. The ships have got bigger and the nature of the cargo has changed. Oil rather than coal is being transported, and the Galicians know only too well the consequences of a shipwreck involving an oil tanker. Although not the first large oil tanker to founder, the ecological damage resulting from the loss of the Prestige in 2002 was the most disastrous. It devastated the precious coastline, its coastal fisheries and, in some cases, the rich seafood beds around the estuaries, including the precious percebes.

One of the few positive consequences of the Prestige disaster was the massive public response, not only in Galicia but across the whole of Spain. Cleaning the beaches became

*Anchor with the Faro do Cabo in the distance (Stage 5)*

a popular obsession, involving coachloads of volunteers, educating thousands on just how delicate the coastal ecosystem is.

## FLORA AND FAUNA

Galicia is favoured by the Gulf Stream and has a warm, wet climate where things grow fast. On the granite cliffs and headlands, heather, gorse, broom and bracken dominate. Where agriculture is retreating, gorse in particular invades and, left alone, soon forms an impregnable barrier. On the dunes, expect to find candy tuft (*iberis procumbens*), sea thrift (*armeria maritima*), cotton weed and, almost unique to this stretch of coast, the carmariñas (*corema album*), a small shrub with a honey-like aroma that grows behind one particular beach.

Broadleaf woodland and pine forests have now sadly given way to eucalyptus over much of Galicia. This was planted initially as an input for the paper industry. Eucalyptus may be seen on the coast but not in the quantities found inland.

The Costa da Morte is a particularly good place to see birds with cliff tops, shallow estuaries and wetlands providing a variety of habitats, ideal for a wide range of permanent

*Clockwise from top left: sea holly at Praia do Treco; spider at work; nasturtiums near Porto de Santa Mariña; insects on cow parsley*

residents and migratory visitors. Nearly 300 species, some very rare, have been seen here. Among the full-time inhabitants are cormorants and shags (if you can tell the difference), the Kentish plover, cloughs and occasionally a peregrine falcon. Among the visitors are sanderlings, swifts, the northern gannet and the Eurasian rock pipit. The shallow estuary of the River Anllóns is a particularly rich environment, sheltered and rich in shellfish, which is ideal for ducks and waders. Its ecosystem has been identified as an important gateway into Europe for birds from North America.

Theoretically, there are some interesting large mammals in Galicia including the already mentioned wolf, brown bears, wild boars and otters, but it's extremely unlikely that you will see any of these. Easier to spot, but exotic to any UK visitor, are red squirrels.

## WHAT'S THE WALKING LIKE?

The walking itself is not challenging. There are no huge ascents or descents, and although there is an occasional a bit of scrambling, it is never dangerous. A few short stretches of cliff-top walking would be unpleasant on a wet windy day and these are highlighted in the detailed route description along with options on how to avoid them in bad weather.

The route, following a well-defined path with good waymarking, is easy to follow. At the time of writing the waymarks are lime green arrows, lime green being colour used in Camiño dos Faros branding. At some point in the near future, these will be replaced by the standard GR white and red markings.

## THE EIGHT DAY SCHEDULE

Although the walking is not difficult, completing the whole 200km in eight days – in line with the Association's schedule – is tough. Some days take 8–9 hours. In developing this guide, alternative schedules have been examined but none of them worked as well as the schedule developed locally, particularly from the perspective of access and accommodation. In addition, given that the excellent Camiño dos Faros website is structured around eight days, presenting this guide in a different way would be confusing.

The good news is that the route is flexible. In particular, while the original tranos were men and women sharing strict principles and sticking rigorously to the coastline, you don't have to. There are many ways to make the route shorter. So if you prefer to have a second glass of Albariño with your lunchtime percebes than it should still be possible to make it to your evening hotel before sunset.

## FOOD AND ACCOMMODATION

Although the Costa da Morte is not at the centre of Spain's huge tourism industry good value accommodation is generally available at the end of each day. There is however no accommodation at the end of the first and fourth stages and taxis need to be organised (although it is possible to walk back across country to accommodation on the first stage). There is a chance that new accommodation may come on stream at the end of Stage 4 so watch out for updates on Cicerone's or the Association's websites.

For most of the year, it isn't necessary to book in advance but people often prefer the reassurance this provides. Spanish hotels seem to like customers to use Booking.com, despite the overhead, and it has the singular advantage of avoiding problems with language.

Food is a key part of the Camiño dos Faros experience, particularly the seafood, and a wide range of restaurants are available. These include simple cafés offering standard fare such as *Pulpo Gallego* (Galician style octopus) all the way through to a lovely Michelin star restaurant halfway through the first day. On some of the days there are places to stop for lunch on the way; on others it is be necessary to take a picnic. Food options are given in the introduction to each stage.

*Clockwise from top left: percebes (goose neck barnacles); vieras a la gallega (Galician scallops); arroz con bogavante (lobster with rice); pulpo a la gallega (octopus Galacian style)*

Festival in Camariñas (Stage 6)

Meals are served late in Spain, and because of its westerly location, it could feel particularly late if you're from the UK. Occasionally, organising timely breakfast or a packed lunch can be a challenge because nothing happens until after the bread delivery.

## PLANNING YOUR WALK

There are three obvious considerations to address when putting together a Camiño dos Faros walking plan: when can you go; how long do you want to take; and, the linked question, whether or not to do all of the walk.

The original tranos started their journey from Malpica to Fisterra in December – in this mild climate it's possible to walk the Camiño dos Faros all year round. It is a wet climate, however, and much of the rain falls in winter. Between October and April, expect rain for 15 days a month. Wet weather is not necessarily a problem but it does change conditions underfoot; some paths become full of water and small streams in the summer become significant obstacles in winter. The very best time to go is late April, May and early June, although it's still fairly dry in July, August and September. Not only will it be colourful with spring flowers but also the light, rain washed and clear, makes for brilliant photographs.

It is worth considering whether to align your schedule with one or more of the many fiestas (refer to Appendix C).

Traski wishes you a good walk

Including getting there and back, you will need a minimum of 10 days to complete the whole of the Camiño dos Faros. The information provided is designed to enable you to construct a schedule to match your own interests and capabilities. Shortcuts are given if you prefer an easier schedule and to help an evaluation of the good and not so good stretches of walking. Two of the eight days involve walking round the main rias: these are less spectacular than the cliff-top walks and, if time is short, could be substituted with a taxi ride.

## GETTING THERE

The two international airports closest to the route are Santiago de Compostela (from London Gatwick or Stansted and most European capitals, with long haul via Madrid or London) and A Coruña (Madrid or London Heathrow). A Coruña is closest to the start of the route and Santiago de Compostela closest to its finish.

If flying into Santiago del Compostela, the best way to get to the start of the route is the train to A Coruña and then the bus to Malpica. Take the airport bus to the train station with trains to A Coruña running at least once an hour and taking around 30 minutes. The bus station in A Coruña is close to the train station and services to Malpica are provided by Transporte Público de Galicia and Arriva (refer to Appendix D). There are up five departures each day, although this varies according to the season and day of the week. There is a bus option to Malpica all the way from Santiago de Compostela but it's more complicated, involves a change, and the service is not that frequent.

If flying into A Coruña, take the airport bus to the bus station and catch the bus to Malpica.

Getting back from Fisterra to Santiago del Compostela is straightforward with Monbus running large coaches from the bus station in the old town five times a day on a journey that takes 3–4 hours.

When planning your travel, consider using the excellent Rome-to-Rio website, which picks up website information from all the main travel operators (www.Rome2Rio.com)

## WHAT TO TAKE

If you are carrying your gear from place to place (taxis can be arranged to carry it for you), then the golden rule is to only take what is needed. Weight is a key consideration and the greater the load, the bigger the strain on your knees and feet. Weigh everything and try to restrict the total load (excluding water) to no more than 7kg.

It shouldn't be cold but it could be wet so pack good quality waterproofs and a waterproof cover for your rucksack.

A comfortable rucksack is an essential item but it's more likely to be comfortable if the total load is only 6–7kg. Stuff sacks within the rucksack might also help; they hardly weigh anything and impose a bit of order when getting packed in the morning.

Footwear should also be light. Remember, 1kg on your feet is equivalent to 4kg on your back. In the summer in particular, avoid heavy boots. Many walkers (myself included) have abandoned boots altogether, opting for 'approach' or fell running shoes instead. Lightweight footwear means your feet stay cooler, your skin is less likely to blister and you can walk further without getting tired.

The Association's website advises long trousers and some of the undergrowth can be a little scratchy. Personally, I prefer to expose my knees whenever I can and on my most recent trip in July, when the undergrowth had reached peak, the skin on my legs survived without too much damage.

## FINDING YOUR WAY

The Camiño dos Faros is not a difficult route to follow but, given the length of some of the days having to retrace your steps after making a wrong turn can be frustrating. The main cause of a wrong turn is likely to be old waymarks dating back to an earlier version of the route which haven't been removed. This shouldn't be a problem in future once the new GR standard waymarks are installed.

Most walkers will not want to rely entirely on waymarks and will want to have their own means of navigation.

Spanish paper maps are not very good and the route is not marked on the map base (generally speaking, footpath information on Spanish maps is limited and not always

*Good waymarking at the beginning of an easy section (Stage 3)*

accurate). If however you decide to buy paper maps, the best way to get hold of them is online from The Mapshop (www.themapshop.co.uk). The maps, provided by IGN, the Spanish National Mapping Agency, are at 1:25,000 scale. Find La Coruna on the Spain Index on The Mapshop website and select:

44 – Sisargas-Carbollo
43 – Lage
67 – Mugia
92 – Finisterre

The maps will then need to be marked up using the information in this guide.

### GPX tracks

Despite the fact that most walkers now have a smartphone, many still don't use the GPS functionality. GPS, however, is the cheapest and most effective way of taking the stress out of navigation. If you already have an Android or Apple smartphone, you can download a GPS app and buy the digital version of the maps listed above from the app's map store.

*Looking west to Cabo Touriñán (Stage 7)*

A recommended app is Viewranger (www.viewranger.com). The Viewranger website includes a map store and a growing portfolio of maps from around the world, including Spain. The Spanish maps are particularly cheap but 'open maps', which don't cost anything, are also available.

The battery on your smartphone should be adequate for a day's walking, particularly if you remember to turn off any features that you're not using. Smartphone GPS doesn't use data roaming so you don't need to have that facility turned on. Phones constantly searching for Wi-Fi also consume energy so turn it and mobile data off. If you are nervous about battery life then take a supplementary battery which can recharge your phone on the move.

GPX tracks for the routes in this guidebook are available to download free at www.cicerone.co.uk/971/GPX. A GPS device is an excellent aid to navigation, but you should also carry a map and compass and know how to use them. GPX files are provided in good faith, but neither the author nor the publisher accept responsibility for their accuracy.

Leaving Malpica (Stage 1)

## USING THIS GUIDE

This guide provides a detailed description of the whole walk broken down into eight stages. Each stage begins by providing basic data including distance, walking time, total ascent and difficulty. There then follows a brief introduction, to provide a feel for the day's walk. Alternative approaches to the walk and shortcuts are also described. Please note that not all the shortcuts have been walked and the description of them may not be as detailed.

The guide should be read in conjunction with the maps. These show all the features highlighted in bold in the text and are designed to help inform what it is you're seeing as you progress along the route. Break-out boxes provide additional information and highlight in context some of the interesting features of the walk.

Please note that place names are taken from the Spanish maps and are in Galego rather than Spanish. This is the convention in Galicia so, for example, instead of Finisterre (the Spanish place name), the guide refers to Fisterra.

# CAMIÑO DOS FAROS

A noisy sea near the Faro do Roncudo (Stage 2)

# STAGE 1

*Malpica to Praia de Niñóns*

| | |
|---|---|
| **Start** | Porto de Malpica |
| **Finish** | Praia de Niñóns (Niñóns Beach) |
| **Distance** | 22km |
| **Ascent** | 740m |
| **Walking time** | 6hr |

Stage 1 is a great introduction to the Camiño dos Faros with the mix of cliff tops and sandy beaches that define the route as a whole. The walk divides neatly into two parts with the second half significantly tougher than the first. Happily, if you're not carrying food, there is also a perfectly positioned lunch stop.

Malpica to As Garzas takes you along low cliffs and round a series of sandy coves. Waymarking is excellent, although it's easy to take a wrong turn in the little villages. The second half takes you along high cliffs to the Punta Nariga and involves some tough walking. The route can be a little overgrown with bracken in the summer. Apart from finding the route through the bracken, which isn't much of a problem, navigation is straightforward.

Stage 1 finishes at the secluded Niñóns Beach and from there you need to pick up a taxi or continue walking. The best place to stay is back at As Garzas where there are two small hotels next to each other. Both are excellent and one of them has a well-deserved Michelin star. Walking back to As Garzas along small country roads, avoiding the cliffs, is about 7km and takes 90 minutes. It's not an unpleasant walk but most people, at the end of long day, order a taxi. If this is your chosen option (the taxi number is provided at the end of the route description), order it before leaving Punta Nariga as telephone reception fizzles out after that. It takes about 60 minutes to walk from the Punta Nariga to Praia de Niñóns.

## ALTERNATIVE SCHEDULES AND SHORTCUTS

There are no obvious shortcuts. If you don't want to walk the whole stage, then missing out the second half, from As Garzas to Praia de Niñóns is the best option. Don't be tempted to tag the second half onto Stage 2, which is already a long day. If you're attracted by the idea of a fabulous meal, book a late lunch at the Michelin starred As Garzas restaurant, spend the rest of the day recovering and then get a taxi to Niñóns Beach in the morning.

## MALPICA

Malpica is the first town on the Camiño dos Faros and a great place to relax before starting the walk. Originally a whaling port (whale vertebrae were used as beams in local houses), it suffered from economic depression as the industry declined with many fishermen leaving for Latin America. Today, its fortunes have revived and it benefits from both a modern fishing industry and tourism, with its sandy beaches making it a popular destination for Spanish families looking for a quiet, reasonably priced holiday. Wandering around the port and old town is an excellent pre-dinner appetiser.

The port is on the eastern side of town and is very informal, with landlubbers and trawlermen intermingling as fish crates and ice are loaded onto boats prior to departure. The piles of nets are huge and irresistible to local children who, perhaps imagining a world of pirates, leap from heap to heap.

*Trawler leaving Malpica*

One street worth visiting in the tightly packed old town is the Rúa Patria Galega where the Camiño dos Faros clubhouse and shop is located. Here you can buy a lime green Camiño T-shirt and a mascot, transforming yourself into a tranos for the duration of the walk.There are plenty of good places to eat. If you like seafood and want to start your trip with an authentic experience than go to the Restauranto O Burato, located in a little side street overlooking the port, the Calle de Eduardo Vila Fana.

Accommodation is plentiful. The Hotel Fonte do Fraile is good and located along the beach on the west side of town (www.hotelfontedofraile.com, tel +34 981 720 732). It you prefer a more central location, consider the Pensión Panchito (www.pensionpanchito.com, tel +34 981 720 307). The hotels are run by members of the same family and resemblance of the sisters involved, identical twins I think, can be seriously confusing. The other centrally located hotel is the Hostal Malpica (www.hostaljbmalpica.com, tel +34 981 721 906).

The Camiño dos Faros starts at the end of the quay in the **Porto de Malpica** at the first, and smallest lighthouse on the whole route. The gate before the stairs up to the lighthouse may be locked, so formally touching the lighthouse to kick the trip off might prove difficult; but on the wall below is the first of many waymarks illuminating the route to Fisterra.

Malpica is built behind a rocky promontory. The port where the Camiño starts is on the promontory's eastern side, and the beach, the **Praia de Area Maior** and route out of town is on its western side. Following the precise route through town is tricky but finding the beach isn't, so you shouldn't get lost.

Continue along the walkway (the Rúa Praia), above the main beach past bars and cafés (the second of these bars, Pub Leno, has the Camiño mascot painted on the wall) to the western edge of town and a smaller beach, the **Praia de Canido**. The hotel, the Fonte do Fraile, is just up the road from here on the left.

Follow a path, initially paved then dirt, up to small walled field above the beach. Turn left and west and after a gentle climb descend down to and around a beach (the **Praia de Seaia**) with picnic tables (and a fountain) at its head. The next target, the Ermita de San Adrián, on the headland ahead, should be clearly visible.

Continue towards the headland on a gently climbing path. On the way the route passes two fountains, the second of the which, **Fonte de San Adrián**, is the most significant. After walking for an hour (4km), the route reaches the **Ermita de San Adrián** where there are excellent views back to Malpica and the three islands of Sisargas.

The chapel on the hill is dedicated to **Saint Adrián** who arrived in the 5th century to get rid of a plague of snakes. He stamped on the first one and the rest disappeared (symbolically, this represents the driving out of pre-Christian pagan cults). The chapel was built in the 16th century and restored in the 20th.

If you're lucky enough to be in Malpica on 16 June, or the nearest Sunday, you'll witness a pilgrimage (*romerias*) where a statue of Saint Adrián is carried shoulder high from a church in the centre of a Malpica up to the chapel. After a service, the many thousands of pilgrims enjoy a picnic feast which, to the accompaniment of Galician pipers, includes the first sardines of the season. After a cockerel auction the statue is carried back into town.

Taking the wart cure at St Adrián's fountain

There are two fountains on the way up to the chapel and the second is the fountain of Saint Adrián. If warts are a problem then bathing in this fountain will provide a cure. Avoid the first fountain however as drinking from this one will give you the flu. The white clothes around Saint Adrián's fountain should be avoided as these have been left there by wart sufferers who have used them to dry themselves after taking the cure.

The route doesn't actually visit the chapel but turns right just beyond a viewing platform and stays close to the coast. Note the standing stone to the right of the chapel. Continue through undergrowth along a wilder path for 200m and, turning west, say goodbye to Malpica. It's your last view of the town. Directly ahead are the **three islands of Sisargas** and on top of the largest one is the first proper lighthouse.

Follow a well-defined path down to a rocky shore, opposite the islands, and continue west. After completing a short climb, and assuming the prevailing westerly wind is blowing, the noise from the sea will suddenly become obvious as you hit the first section of west-facing coast. Ahead, at the end of the Punta Nariga, is the day's third lighthouse, the Faro de Punta Nariga, our penultimate target. Continue along a beautifully contouring path that hovers above little bays. Depending on the season, watch out for house martins (white breast) nesting in the low cliffs.

The **Sisargas Islands** ('Grande', 'Chica' and 'Malante') are important sanctuaries for seabirds with various levels of protected status. They play host to colonies of black backed gulls (the largest member of the gull family), kittiwakes and the Caspian gull. The common guillemot was endemic to these islands but since the Prestige oil tanker disaster, they only stopover on their migration.

In the summer, the islands take on a pink tinge caused by the flowering of a carpet of sea thrift.

The islands also host the first proper lighthouse on the Camiño dos Faros. It is one of the oldest on the route and was built in 1853, upgraded in 1919, and has been running automatically since 2002. The islands can be visited (there is a little pier), but only by organising a boat in Malpica.

As the path swings south around the peninsula (the Cabo de San Adrián) the land opens up, the cliffs fizzle out, and the path becomes a track. Ahead is the village of **Seiruga**.

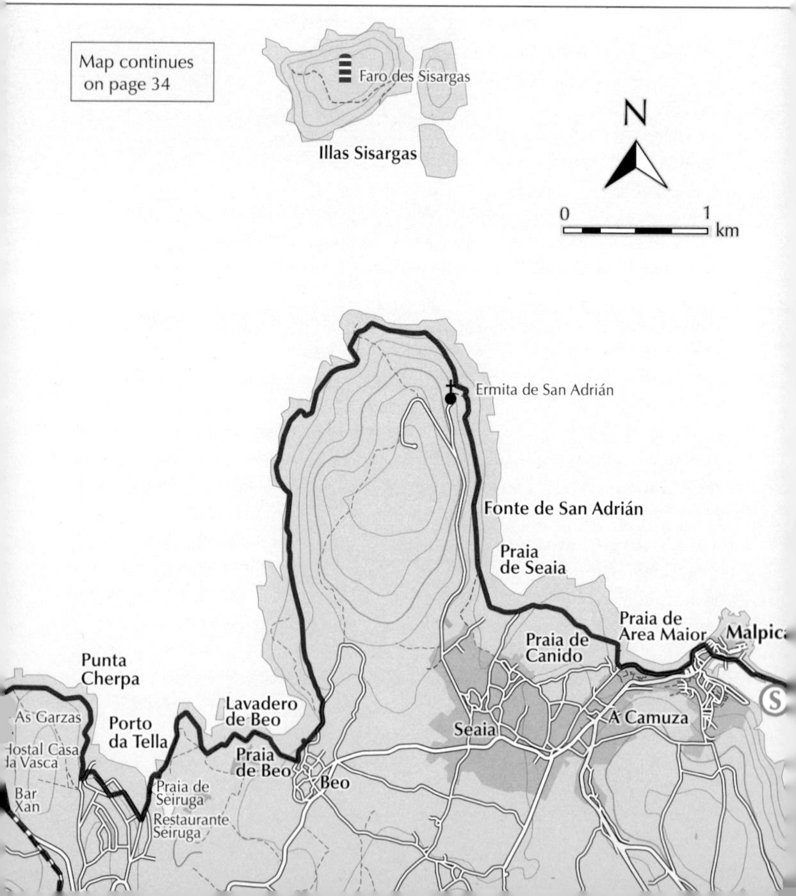

*Looking back to Sisargas*

Continue south to an important junction 3km from Ermita de San Adrián. Ignore the path heading towards the coast (an old and now dangerous path) and stick with the track heading directly south. Follow the track through dense vegetation over a low shoulder to a road with a tarmac surface and turn right.

Just before the village of Beo, the first **eucalyptus trees** are encountered. Planted in the Franco era to support the paper industry, huge and largely unmanaged forests now blight the Galician countryside. Despite high annual rainfall, the combustible nature of eucalyptus makes the region the most prone to forest fires.

Follow the road down the hill, towards the village of **Beo**. Turn right after 100m, head down to the beach (**Praia de Beo**), and follow the waymarks past the picnic tables and up the zigzagging steps to the village.

Turn right onto the road in the village, continue for 100m, and then turn right again returning to the coast. Keep to the left of a surprisingly modern house and head down the hill past a stone cross. Continue down to the sea passing the old village laundry (**Lavadero de Beo**) on the way. After 100m leave the track and join a path that runs close to the sea. Rejoin the track and follow it west behind a fisherman's hut and a small natural harbour (**Porto da Tella**). Join a tarmac road, follow it for 200m and turn right. After 100m on tarmac, turn right onto a dirt track and follow it round the low headland to the next beach (**Praia de Seiruga**).

On the eastern side of the beach, a stream enters the sea. Depending on the time of the year and the tide this can present an obstacle. In April, shoes may have to be removed and trousers rolled up (or worse) before wading across the stream. In July, it shouldn't be a problem.

Head up the beach to a white bar/restaurant, the Seiruga, and leave the tarmac road and join a dirt track just beyond it on the right. Turn left onto a path after 200m and climb a steep sandy bank. Turn right onto a tarmac road and then immediately right. After you pass the last house, join a path, follow it down to a tarmac road, turn left onto it and then right and then sharp right onto a path. The route is working its way round another beautiful little beach.

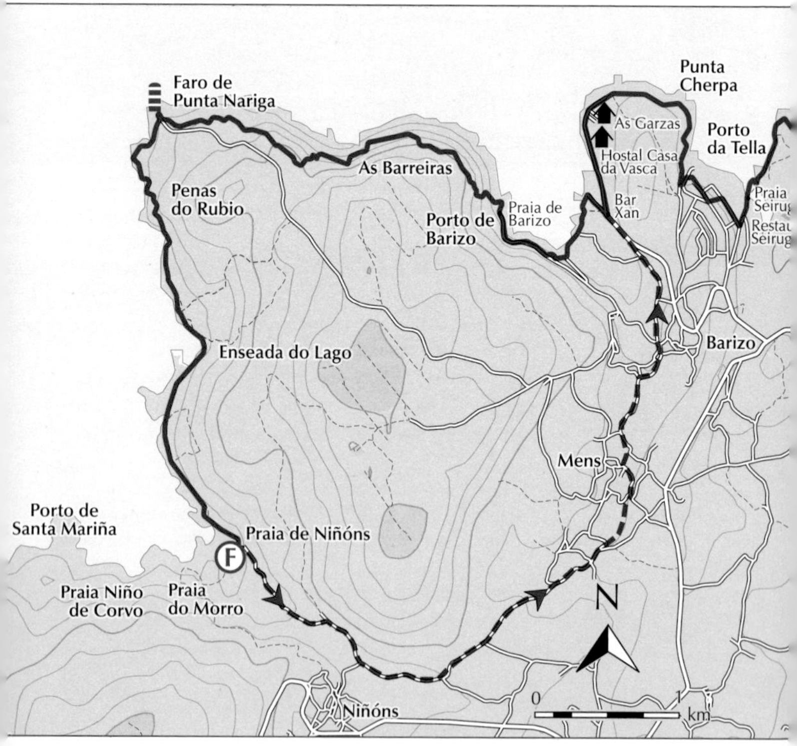

Follow a well-defined path through gorse and bracken along the east side of a headland (**Punta Cherpa**). Watch out for cormorants or shags, sunning themselves on the rock below. Continue along a lovely path through heather and gorse around the headland. Out on the rocks you'll probably see fishermen chancing their luck among the crashing waves. The good walking comes to an abrupt ends and, passing some sort of treatment works, the route joins a tarmac road. Immediately on the left is the **Casa da Vasca**, and next to it the **As Garzas**. If you're staying at either of these places, it makes sense to drop some weight before continuing with a smaller load to Niñóns Beach.

On the western side of the peninsula is a distributed settlement around As Garzas where, in an otherwise empty area, a wide range of culinary tastes are catered for. A popular lunch stop for local workers is the Restaurant O Xan down the road on the corner, where, if something quick is needed, a sandwich can be bought. The Pensión Rústica Casa da Vasca is a small hotel that also has a restaurant (www.casadavasca.com, tel +34 981 721 960). Next door to the hotel is the As Garzas, with its Michelin starred restaurant (www.asgarzas.com, tel +34 981 720 605). The As Garzas also provides rooms. On our first trip to the Camiño, we enjoyed a long boozy lunch (starting at 2.30pm), abandoned the rest of the day's walk and stayed there.

Continue for 800m along the road, turn right then take a sharp left along a path next to a concrete wall, just before the Bar Xan. Follow the path down to the **Praia de Barizo**, a beach with particularly white sand. Cross the beach and follow a ramp up a car turning area. At the seaward side of the area is a path – follow it and climb steeply up to the road. Turn right onto the road and follow it down to the very modern fishing sheds below, in the **Porto de Barizo**. Continue past the slipway, and past a lamppost with red-and-white footings, to join a path to the left of railings. Follow the path on a steep and rocky climb through deep bracken up the side of the hill.

Once you're on the top, there is a long stretch of walking through what, in summer, feels like a bracken tunnel (depending on your height). At times the path is a little exposed but never dangerously so. After about 1km, the path turns slightly and, with a suddenly open vista, you'll see the lighthouse – the Faro de Punta Nariga – for the first time.

The next milestone is **As Barrieras** (138m), a wind blasted lump of granite like a tor on Dartmoor, which you'll reach after completing a short but stiff climb. Passing through a little rock window, continue into what is now a rocky landscape. After another 100m of relatively level walking, the lighthouse pops up again, and suddenly it feels close. It's deceptive though, and although it's downhill nearly all

On a wet day heading to the Faro de Punta Nariga

the way it takes another 20 minutes or so to cross what is a rocky divide to reach the lighthouse. The Camiño does not give time off for good behaviour and despite the availability of a tempting access road, sticks to the cross country route all the way to the **Faro de Punta Nariga**.

The route's most modern lighthouse, and the first big one visited, the **Faro de Punta Nariga** only started operation in 1998. It's built to resemble a boat and a bronze statue by Manola Coia sits in its 'bows', challenging the crashing waves below.

Following the earlier sighting of eucalyptus, another invasive plant features at the Punta Nariga – this time it's the brightly coloured succulent, the sour fig (*Carpobrotus Edulis*), originally from South Africa and now an unwanted guest outstaying any welcome on coastlines around the world.

*Looking north to the Faro de Punta Nariga*

The next stretch of coastline is once more facing west, happily too windy for the bracken and usually featuring some spectacular waves. Find a path at the lighthouse end of the car park and follow it southwest downhill. After descending to a rocky shoreline, climb over a saddle, the **Penas do Rubio**, before dropping steeply onto an open and almost flat terrain.

Follow the path round a pretty stony bay, **Enseada do Lago**, to a track serving a couple of isolated fisherman's buildings. Continue along what is now an easy track to the beach, **Praia de Niñóns**. There's not much there but it's a good place to pick up a taxi.

## NOTE

If you wish to get a taxi back from Praia de Niñóns to your accommodation in As Garzas, I'd recommend Luis Busto (tel +34 606 400 932) or Enrique (tel +34 610 654 815).

# STAGE 2

*Praia de Niñóns to Ponteceso*

| | |
|---|---|
| **Start** | Praia de Niñóns |
| **Finish** | Ponte de Ponteceso |
| **Distance** | 26km |
| **Ascent** | 510m |
| **Walking time** | 7hr 45min |

Stage 2 is long and includes a wide variety of beautiful but often tough coastal walking. It has everything: massive cliffs, secluded bays, fishing harbours, beaches and sand spits.

The day starts with a remote stretch of walking along north-facing cliffs before heading south and around Camiño's first major west-facing peninsula (the Punta do Roncudo). Travelling inland to the port of Corme, the path gets easier and the pace picks up but the respite turns out to be short-lived. Beyond Corme and its harbour and beaches, with the route now heading south and the coastline facing west, another stretch of tough coastal walking bars the way to your destination. The final part of the walk, heading east into the ria and towards Ponteceso, is easier but, unless you're a very fast walker, the sun could now be low in the sky.

Stage 2 can be completed in the daylight and if the weather is good it will be a truly memorable experience. Many people, however, will want to consider shortcuts or alternative schedules.

There is nowhere to buy lunch until Corme, and getting there even in time for a late Spanish lunch is a challenge so, unless you can arrange an early departure, consider taking a picnic.

## ALTERNATIVE SCHEDULES AND SHORTCUTS

It's difficult to recommend dropping any of Stage 2 because, apart from a stretch of road from the Faro do Roncudo to O Porte de Corme, it's all good. The most obvious alternative schedule involves splitting the stage in two and finishing the first part at Port de Corme. O Porte de Corme is actually slightly larger than Ponteceso and, providing you're not there on a Sunday night early in the season, there are places to eat. Accommodation, however, is limited to a block of self-catering apartments that don't always cater for single night bookings in the holiday season. If accommodation isn't available, then spending two nights at Ponteceso or As Garzas and using taxis to make the connections is the best solution.

Given the shape of the coastline, there is one obvious shortcut. Instead of going to Faro do Roncudo and round the peninsula, head directly south to O Porte de Corme through the little village of O Roncudo. This saves around 4km – about an hour – and avoids a stretch along the road, but it means dropping a particularly lovely part of the coast on the approach to the lighthouse.

Perhaps the best option, if the weather is settled, is to pack double rations and get going earlier than normal – Stage 3 is a lot easier!

Head around the **Praia de Niñóns** to a stream, follow it inland and cross it just before an old watermill. Follow a gently climbing path through eucalyptus trees (ignoring a turn to the left), take a right turn after 400m and descend back down to a beach (the **Praia do Morro**). Turn left before the beach (apparently a nudist beach) and continue above it along the coast. There are occasional turn offs from the path, that can be overgrown with bracken, but the correct path sticks close to the coast. Note how eucalyptus has taken over from pine.

Swinging around a low headland, the path emerges from the trees above a small beach, the **Praia de Niño do Corvo**. You should now be able to see the low huts of **Porto de Santa Mariña** ahead. Continue along the coast to a road and follow it into the port.

Cross the car park and bear left, head to rocks immediately above the sea and follow a now open path that sticks limpet-like to the coastline. Around 600m from the car park, and after passing a stone cross, head through a fence, turn inland and follow the path up a shallow valley. Ignore tempting paths to the right, continue for 400m (now heading southeast) to a road and turn right. The noise of the sea will now have disappeared and, apart from birdsong, everything will be suddenly quiet.

Continue south along the road for 300m and take a right turn onto a path lined with slabs of stone. Markings on the road show the turn clearly. Follow the path as it climbs gently and then levels out into an expanse of broom. The end of the climb is marked by a ridge of low summits including one called **O Bravío**. The view from the ridge into the sheltered bay below, the **Enseada da Barda**, is excellent. The walk around the bay, however, takes a surprisingly long time.

From the ridge, follow the path on a steep descent that almost makes it to the shoreline before turning inland. This path can be slippery when the weather is wet.

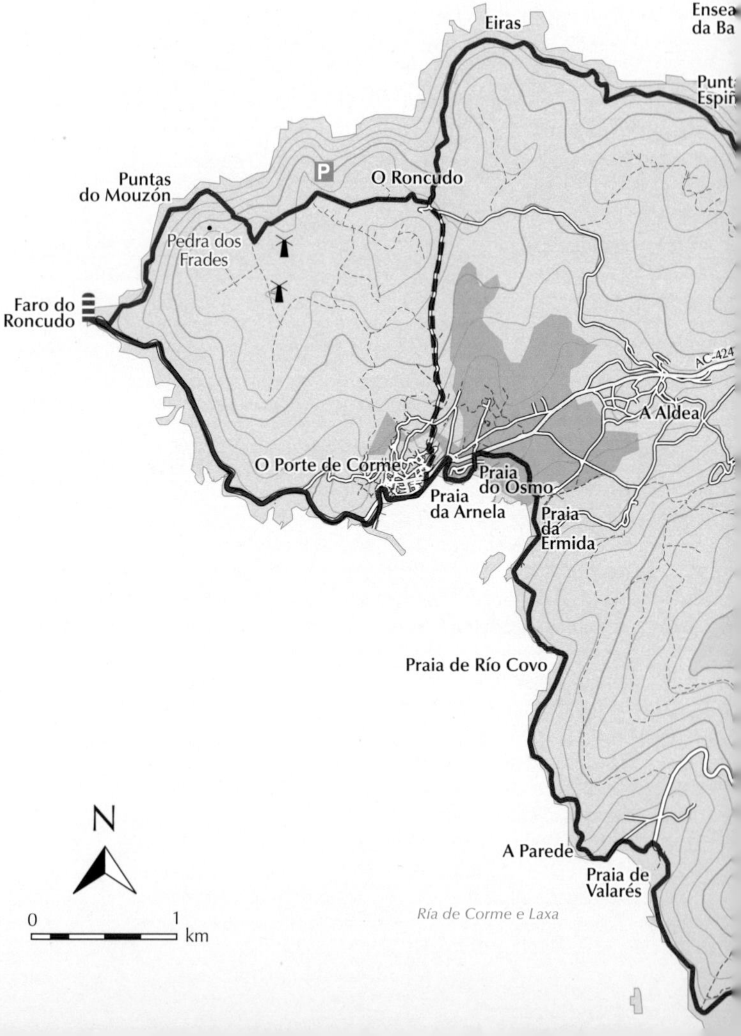

Eiras
Ensea
da Ba
Punt
Espiñ
Puntas
do Mouzón
P
O Roncudo
Pedra dos
Frades
Faro do
Roncudo
AC-424
A Aldea
O Porte de Corme
Praia
do Osmo
Praia
da Arnela
Praia
da
Ermida
Praia de Río Covo
A Parede
Praia de
Valarés
Ría de Corme e Laxa
N
0
1
km

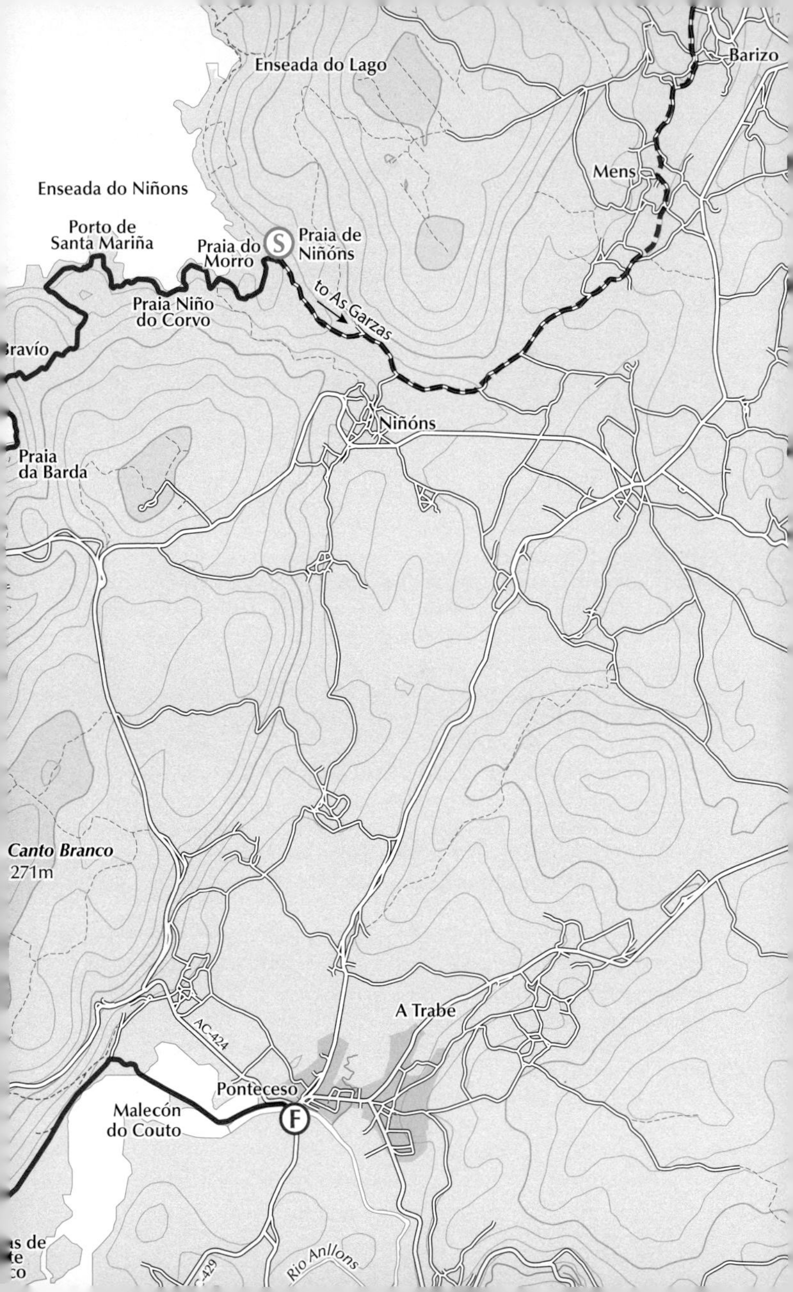
Enseada do Lago
Barizo
Mens
Enseada do Niñons
Porto de Santa Mariña
Praia do Morro
S
Praia de Niñóns
Praia Niño do Corvo
to As Garzas
Bravío
Niñóns
Praia da Barda
Canto Branco
271m
AC-424
A Trabe
Ponteceso
Malecón do Couto
F
AC-429
Río Anllons

*On the Praia da Barda*

Continue inland along a level but usually overgrown path before emerging onto a stunning little beach, the **Praia da Barda**. Although the beach will almost certainly be empty, fishermen clearly value its sheltered position and a few boats, bobbing gently on the swell, will be moored nearby. Cross the beach and follow the path up a tiny dilapidated slipway. The path emerges onto a road. Follow it up the hill for 50m and join a path to the right. Head down to a tiny stream, bear right and follow the path through dense undergrowth across wet ground. Fortunately the path soon dries out as it takes a gently ascending route along the west side of the cove. After reaching an outcrop of rock marking the entrance to the bay, the path turns west and climbs steeply to the top of the cliffs, the **Punta Espiñeira**.

Continue west along an increasingly dramatic and generally less overgrown cliff-top path. Watch out for the lonely little cross perched right on the edge. Staying high, with the few small valleys running into sea presenting just minor barriers, your progress west should now be faster.

Head west to a gnarled and weathered outcrop of crops known as **Eiras**. This marks the point where the coast turns south. Just before you reach them, looking back, you should be able to see two lighthouses, the Faro de Punta Nariga and behind that the Faros des Sisargas. Just beyond Eiras, as the path swings south (and becomes much easier), the next target the village of **O Roncudo**, apparently guarded by wind turbines, comes into view.

Follow a level path south, which starts to climb as it heads inland on the final approach to village. Continue through the village, turning right next to a shed with a cross protruding from its asbestos roof. If you want to take the shortcut to O Porte de Corme (saving about an hour), stay on the road and head south through the village.

**O Roncudo** looks like a place built for windy, wet weather. The squat stone houses, with roof tiles secured with stone, look like inviting places to shelter in and hide from the rain. One of the occupants, however, clearly has a sunny disposition and has painted his house an exceptionally bright turquoise. A sense of pride is also evident in the fields close to village, which are densely farmed with multiple crops – maize, beans and tomatoes.

Follow a road west out of the village and take the right-hand fork after about 600m. The road ends in a grassy car park and the path leaves it at its western end. After passing some beautifully weathered columns of stone, follow the path across a rocky moorland west-southwest. A wind turbine with a well-placed waymark signals a sharp turn right. Continue northwest across the moorland then start a steep descent towards the sea. Ahead to the left are some extravagantly weathered lumps of granite (the **Pedra dos Frades**), which remind me at least of a Gaudí building.

Nearing the end of the descent, turn left to start an exceptional and probably noisy stretch of coastal walking. There are views all the way back to the Sisargas Islands and ahead, across a huge bay, towards tomorrow's target Cabo Laxe. After rounding a corner and crossing a low saddle – the **Puntas do Mouzón** – the Faro do Roncudo (the little lighthouse at the end of the peninsula), suddenly comes into view, and although it takes another 20 minutes to reach it, every step is a treat.

What the **Faro do Roncudo** lacks in height (it's only 11m tall), it makes up for in location. Built at the end of a low promontory in 1920, it enjoys the most amazing views across the Ria de Corme south and on to Laxe. The name 'roncudo' derives from the Galician word for snore, and the steady rumble of the waves is said to resemble the noise made by a large man sleeping on his back.

*Faro do Roncudo*

Follow the path to within a few metres of the **lighthouse** and the start of some easy walking. The route from the lighthouse to **O Porte de Corme** involves a fairly mindless 3km walk along a road. If you've timed things right and get there before 3.30pm, you could reward yourself with a plate of percebes and a chilled glass of Albariño.

## PERCEBES

I was introduced to *percebes* by chance in Santander a few weeks before my first Camiño dos Faros trek. An enthusiastic and patient restaurateur explained how to eat them (a sort of pinch and pull technique) and what wine to drink with them (a delicious Galician white wine made from the Godello grape). Amazingly, just a few weeks later, I found myself in the world's percebes capital, O Porte de Corme.

Percebes are special creatures. Each resembling a tiny claw, they grow clinging onto wave washed rocks among breaking waves. Harvesting them involves special fishermen who, clad in wetsuits and attached to the shoreline by a rope, hack away among the surf and rocks filling little buckets with this special delicacy. It's a dangerous process and the crosses on the coast near the Faro do Roncudo mark places where fishermen have perished.

The taste and the challenging harvesting process makes them expensive, although O Porte de Corme (and the Costa da Morte in general) is the best and cheapest place to eat them: much cheaper than Santander.

O Porte de Corme has carefully cultivated its association with percebes and, since the earlier 1990s, on the first Saturday of July, has hosted a percebes festival. This has become the most important annual gastronomic event in the province of Coruna, and attracts foodies from all over the world.

Finding anything open early in the season in Porto de Corme is a challenge and the busy times, when the town was one of Spain's biggest wood exporting ports, are now long gone. Despite cultivating its association with percebes, the fishing industry has not managed to recover as it has in Malpica. There is accommodation in the form of self-catering apartments (Apartamentos Turísticos Playa de Osmo, www.playadeosmo.com, tel +34 981 705 278). These might be hard to book for just one night in the summer.

Follow the seafront walkway to the first of the town's beaches, the **Praia da Arnela**. On the other side of beach, climb a low flight of steps and continue on the walkway underneath plane trees and past picnic tables. The holiday flats (Apartamentos Turísticos Playa de Osmo) are located next to this walkway.

*Looking back to O Porte de Corme*

Follow the walkway to its end and the next town beach, the **Praia do Osmo**, and turn left up a road, turn right onto a main road and right again after 10m. Continue along this side street to a path and follow it down into pine trees. After crossing a bridge, continue with the path over a saddle to another beach, the **Praia da Ermida**. It's an excellent path, waymarked with local footpath signs.

When you reach the beach, turn right and cross it (ignoring the local signs). Aim for the bridge over a stream on the other side of the beach and join a track just beyond it. Follow the track over a low headland facing a small island. After a brief inland excursion over a saddle the route returns to the coast, crosses a gully behind a small beach (**Praia de Río Covo**) and then follows an undulating path for next 2km. An interesting path, it spends most of its time about 20m above the sea and 20m below the top of cliffs. This is a strategy that works until the cliffs get vertical, at which point defeat is conceded and the path is forced to turn inland and climb. After a short but sharp climb, you will arrive at a heavily weathered rock platform, known as '**A Parede**' (the wall), which provides wonderful views up the coast. Continue south until the west-facing cliffs come to a sudden end and the path turns east on a steep descent. Ahead, you will now see Ponteceso, although unfortunately it's not as close as it looks.

**THE TITANIUM YEARS**

Locals remember with considerable fondness the brief titanium boom, the mining of which provided employment from 1936 to the early 1960s at a time when the rest of Spain was enduring considerable poverty. The deposit, discovered by Isidro Parga Pondal, son of Eduardo Pondal (see below) was exhausted by the 1960s. The buildings at the Praia de Valarés, and the harbour wall, were used to export the titanium and once the ore had finished the facilities were used by local smugglers to import tobacco among other things.

After reaching a weird crab-like sculpture at the end of a breakwater, turn left and head round the beach, the **Praia de Valarés**. Continue to a car park and roundabout at the rear of a second part of the beach, and after briefly following duckboards turn left and head to a local footpath sign. The beaches, with campsites nearby, are particularly popular with families. Turn right and follow the white-and-yellow signs towards trees and a low headland. Ignore a right turn up a steep sandy path despite the green marker on a tree. This is an old route that goes over the Petón da Farola and following it would be an unwelcome distraction at the end of a long day.

*On the edge of the huge sand spit*

Continue south along low cliffs for about 1.8km and then turn sharp left and follow a track crossing the inland side of a large sandbar, the **Dunas de Monte Branco**, on the northern bank of the River Anllóns estuary. Continue inland for nearly 2km, leaving the track just beyond a metal barrier. Turn right and follow an embankment (the **Malecón do Couto**), mostly along a boarded path that separates the estuary from wetlands. Follow this path all the way to **Ponteceso**.

## EDUARDO PONDAL

Opposite the bridge on the corner of the road is a large elegant house, the birthplace in 1835 of Eduardo Pondal. A Galician nationalist and poet, Eduardo was a central figure in 19th century attempts to create a distinct Galician identity. Writing in Galego, he idealises a past where a Celtic population fought a Roman invader and projects this onto a contemporary domination by Castilian Spain. Words from his poem *Queixume dos Pinos*, together with the music by Pascual Veiga, are part of the Galician anthem. Eduardo loved the Galician countryside and a local footpath, the Pondaliana Route, has been created that visits places referred to in his poetry. The monolith in the main square is the first of 14 that mark the route and the poet's profile points towards the direction of travel.

*Pontecesco*

## PONTECESO

Ponteceso is a small town that enjoys a full range of services (chemist, supermarket and banks) and most importantly a hotel, the Pensión Teyma. To find it, go east down the main shopping street, turn left at the junction at its end, and continue up the road for 200m to the hotel (on the left). It's a modest but good value hotel and features a restaurant/bar that serves quick food (www.pensionteyma.com, tel +34 981 715 404).

# STAGE 3

*Ponteceso to Laxe*

| | |
|---|---|
| **Start** | Ponte de Ponteceso |
| **Finish** | Plaza Ramón Juega |
| **Distance** | 25km |
| **Ascent** | 430m |
| **Walking time** | 6hr 35min |

Stage 3 is long but most of the walking is fast and easy. If needed, there is a simple way to make it shorter.

The first part of the day, a stroll along the southern bank of the River Anllóns estuary, is as flat as a pancake and very relaxing. The second part involves an inland detour to visit two important archaeological sites, the Castro A Cibda and the Dólmen de Dombate, and includes a sharp climb up the Castelo de Lourido (312m), the highest point in the whole route. Returning to the coast, the third part involves a lovely stretch of low cliff-top walking that finishes at the beach in front of Laxe. The route is well marked and simple to follow although there are stretches on the third part that can be overgrown. There is a well-positioned café to stop for an early lunch but Castelo de Lourido also provides a stunning location for a picnic stop.

## ALTERNATIVE SCHEDULES AND SHORTCUTS

The obvious shortcut, and easy to execute, involves missing the inland visit to Castro A Cibda and the Dólmen de Dombate. While both sites are interesting, particularly Castro A Cibda, it can be argued (if you need an excuse to take a shortcut after a massive Stage 2) that the inland excursion is out of character with what is otherwise a coastal walk. To take the shortcut, instead of heading inland along the Rego dos Muiños, go west along the main road up a hill for 400m, past the Bar O Cruceiro, to rejoin the route as it returns from its visit to the Castelo de Lourido. This will save you 1hr 50min.

From the centre of **Ponteceso**, cross Ponte de Ponteceso and follow the footpath along the road up a gentle hill. Cross the road about 100m past the kilometre marker and follow a side street (gardens with railings on the right) downhill into pine trees. At the last house leave the tarmac and join a path.

Follow the path through mixed woodland, turn right onto a gravel road and, ignoring a left hand fork after 600m, head downhill. Just before you reach the estuary, turn left and continue through trees along a path running parallel to the water. Continue through trees to a road, reached after 1km, turn right and head down to the estuary and along the coast to the **Praia da Urixeira**. If you're lucky with the tide, instead of following the path through the trees, you can walk along the shore.

## ESTUARIO DE ANLLÓNS

The Estuario de Anllóns is one of a series estuaries known collectively as the Rías Gallegas that form internationally important feeding and resting grounds for a rich variety of wildfowl and waders that breed in northern Europe, Russia or the high Arctic, and winter in Spain, or pass through to winter in Africa. Its position on the western edge of Europe makes Galicia a hotspot for rare North American waterfowl vagrants who, blown in by gales, turn up with some regularity. The Estuario de Anllóns, and the wetlands and lagoon behind the sandbank, has a particular reputation for hosting such strays.

The sandbank itself is a special feature, a huge dune 2km long and 400m wide that almost closes the estuary. Although moving, it is anchored to a degree by plant life, some of which (notably the endangered *Omphalodes Littorralis Galleacica*) is unique to this location.

*The sand bar at the Anllóns Estuary*

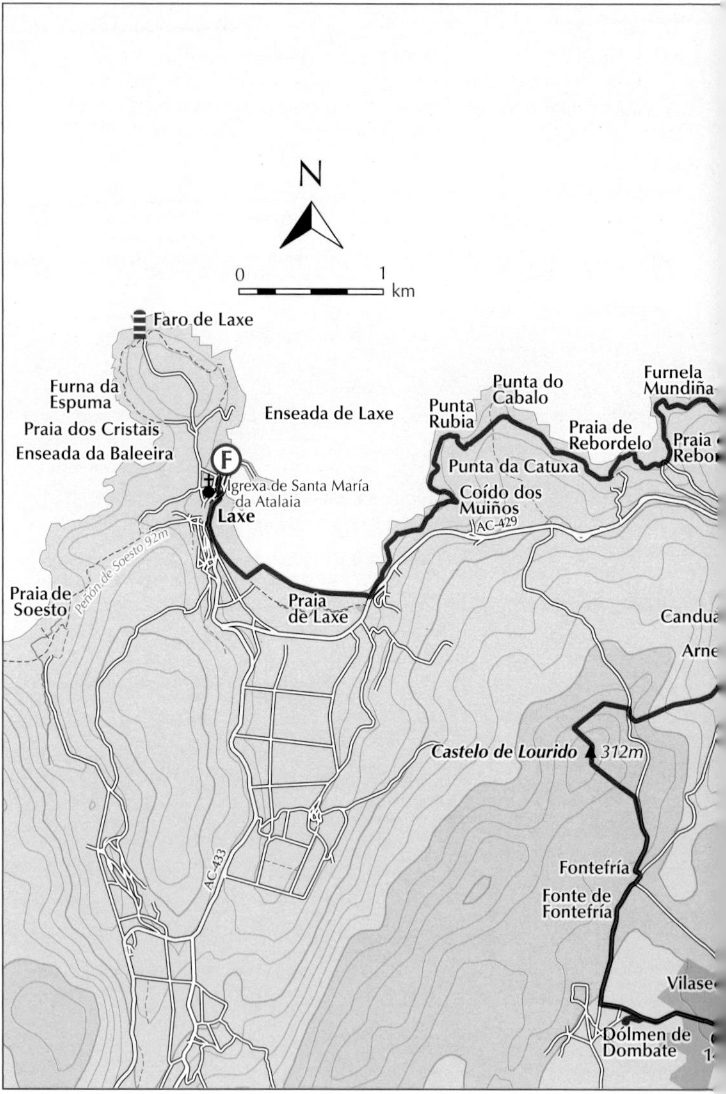
N
0
1
km
Faro de Laxe
Furna da Espuma
Praia dos Cristais
Enseada da Baleeira
Enseada de Laxe
F
Igrexa de Santa María da Atalaia
Laxe
Peñon de Soesto 92m
Praia de Soesto
Praia de Laxe
AC-429
AC-433
Punta Rubia
Punta do Cabalo
Punta da Catuxa
Coído dos Muiños
Praia de Rebordelo
Furnela Mundiña
Castelo de Lourido
312m
Fontefría
Fonte de Fontefría
Dólmen de Dombate

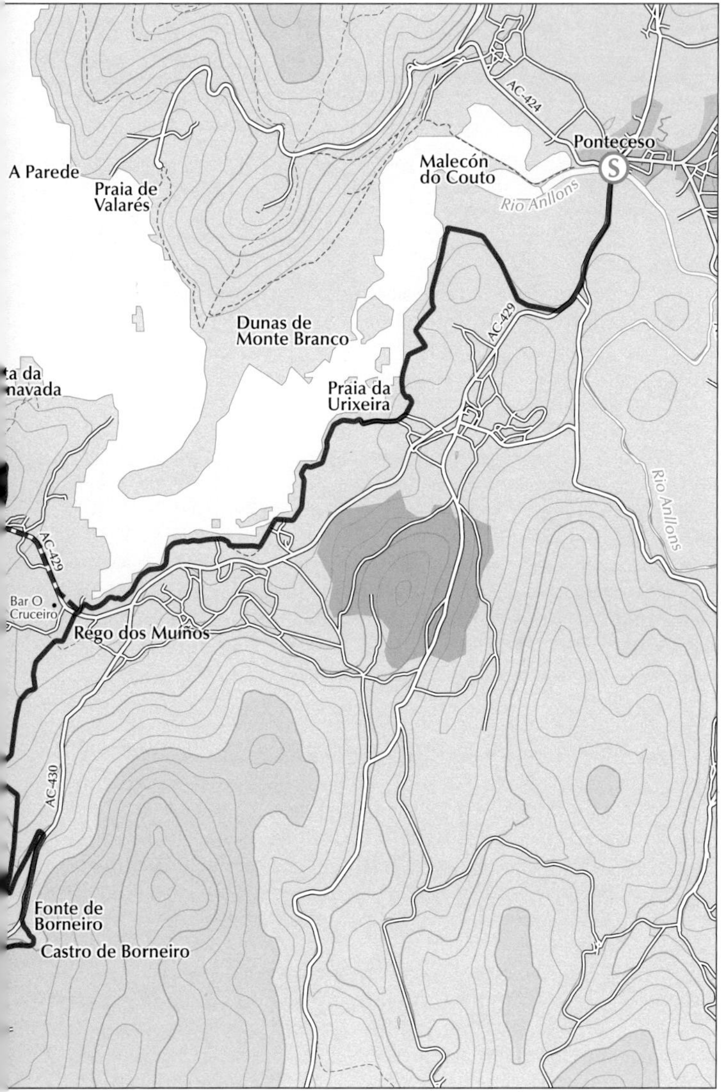
AC-424
Ponteceso
S
Malecón
do Couto
Río Anllons
A Parede
Praia de
Valarés
Dunas de
Monte Branco
AC-429
Praia da
Urixeira
ta da
navada
Río Anllons
AC-429
Bar O
Cruceiro
Rego dos Muíños
AC-430
Fonte de
Borneiro
Castro de Borneiro

On the other side of the beach, the route joins what must be one of world's most perfectly engineered riverside walks, the Sendero de Anllóns, a 3km surfaced path along the edge of the estuary. It's a very pleasant walk with no navigational challenges and evolving views of the estuary and its abundant birdlife. If the weather is good, the Galicians – young and old – will also come out to play.

The path finally ends opposite a small shipyard and some granite benches. Head up to a main road (the **AC-429**), cross it and follow a path initially on duckboards heading inland. To make the shortcut head west along the main road up a hill for 400m, past the Bar O Cruceiro. You are now at the start of the Ruta do Rego Dos Muíños and an information board on the left describes what the walk is all about. The first mill is reached after 100m. A few metres up the road on the right is a recommended lunch stop spot, the **Bar O Cruceiro**.

After 600m the duckboard turns into a gravel path. It's an easy path to follow and the variety of trees – birch, silver birch, beech, oak and sweet chestnut, as well as the ever present eucalyptus – adds to the enjoyment. Continue on this for 2.5km, to a junction with a dirt road. Follow the dirt road as it swings north and up to a surprisingly large road (**AC-430**), turn right and head up the road for 600m to a car park on the road's left hand side. At the back of the car park is a fountain, the **Fonte de Borneiro**, next to which is a track and a sign to Castro de Borneiro. Follow it for a few metres to another mill and join a path immediately behind it. Continue along the path up the valley where suddenly you're confronted with the outer wall of the **Castro de Bornerio** itself. Walk through the circular stoneworks and follow the route out via a viewing platform. Turn right onto a track, head down to the main road (AC-430), turn left and cross the road after a few metres. Go down a side road and the Ruta Megalítica into the village of **Vilaseco**.

More a fortified village than a castle, the **Castro A Cibdá Borneiro** shows how the population lived in Galicia before the Roman invasion. It was discovered in 1924 by Isidro Parga Pondal, the great nephew of Eduardo Pondal, and excavated in the 1930s. Contained within walls are a series of stone circles, the remains of circular houses, demonstrating that this was a Celtic rather than Roman settlement. The remains suggest a sophisticated society. As well as houses the village contains a blacksmith, stables and even a sauna.

Follow the road up through the village to a bus stop sponsored by the Caixa Galicia (ignore markings sending you along an old version of the route) and continue along the road, taking the next right and then right again at the junction. Continue away from the houses (and barking dogs) down to a larger road (**CP-1404**) and turn right. Follow the road down to the **Dólmen de Dombate**.

## DOLMEN DE DOMBATE

Much older than the Castro A Cibdá Borneiro, older even than Stonehenge in the UK, is the Dólmen de Dombate. Constructed between 3800 and 3600BC (and featuring in the poetry of Eduardo Pondal), the Dolmen is considered a Galician 'megalithic cathedral'. It is in fact part of a burial mound, and would originally have been covered by earth – and there are examples of similar features all over the world. The Dólmen de Dombate is a particularly good example and consists of a central chamber comprising seven stone slabs (orthostats) approached via a corridor leading from the entrance. The chamber has some wall paintings, and when the site was excavated in the 1980s a row of idols was discovered. The Dolmen is now the central feature of a covered interpretation centre. Entrance is free but the centre is closed from 2–4pm and the information boards provide no concessions to those of us who only speak English.

*Dólmen de Dombate*

Return to the road, turn left and go west to a mini-roundabout. Turn right and follow the road past the *lavedeiro* (communal washing) and fountain to the village of **Fontefría**. After ignoring an initial left turn at the edge of the village, take a left fork at the next junction followed by another two left turns to emerge onto a concrete road. Turn right and follow this road as it goes north out the village. After 600m leave the road and turn left onto a forest path. Ignore an immediate turn to the left and continue climbing through the forest to the summit of **Castelo de Lourido**.

The views from the **Castelo de Lourido** are impressive. The huge meander visible in Estuario de Anllóns confirms its status as a flooded river valley (or ria). To the northwest, Laxe and its peninsula should also be visible.

Head northwest (towards Laxe in the distance) and follow a steeply descending path from the summit. After 150m, turn right onto a nearly level path. Follow this for 200m and then take a right fork swinging to the southeast. Continue down to a road (the same road from which we started the ascent to Castelo de Lourido), turn left (onto the road) and, after a few metres, turn right onto a track. Follow this track all the way to the tiny village of **Arnela** carefully avoiding a left turn after 400m where some old waymarks could tempt a digression.

Take a sharp right at the junction in the centre of the Arnela (marked with a cross) and follow the road north towards the coast and the dispersed village of **Canduas**. Bear left at the first junction immediately inside the settlement (the one with a stop sign). Continue up the hill between two precipitously positioned *hórreo*. Ignore a left-hand turn and follow the road to another junction marked by a stop sign, then turn left.

The inland excursion provides numerous examples of **hórreo**, corn-drying stores characteristic of villages in Galicia and the Asturias. Some of them, including those in Canduas, enjoy dramatic locations. Their slotted sides means that they are ventilated by the wind but protected from the rain. Their construction, on a protruding ledge supported by narrow pillars, is designed to make them rat-proof. They vary in size but the biggest one in Galicia is 35m long.

Follow the road to a junction with a main road, the AC-429, the same road crossed a few hours ago on the way up to Dólmen de Dombate. It's not back to square one, not quite anyway. From the other side of the main road, follow a steeply climbing tarmac road past houses into beautiful tall pine trees. After 500m, turn left on a forest track down past a small house with a blue cable car in the garden. The sea, once again, should now be within earshot.

Ignore two left-hand turns and follow the track through bracken down to low cliffs (**Punta da Escanavada**). At this point leave the track and join a path. The path, which could be overgrown, climbs as it makes it way round a cove. For the next 400m follow an easy path (relatively flat) all the way to a little headland (the **Furnela Mundiña**) before turning to descend to the **Praia de Rebordelo**. The path goes around the head of the beach but a more direct route across the sand is likely to prove irresistible. If you've crossed the beach aim for rocks in the far corner over which a stream is dropping into the sea. Depending on the time of year, this stream will either be a dribble or a full blown waterfall.

Early season waterfall at the Praia de Rebordelo

Climb up from the beach and follow the path round the next shallow headland, the **Punta da Catuxa**, to another beautiful secluded beach, (the Praia de San Pedro). Don't attempt to cross the beach but stick with the path around it as there is no way up the cliffs on its other side. After the second beach the path stays high but close to sea. It's good walking but can be little overgrown. Cutting across the next headland, (the **Punta do Cabalo**), via the Pedra do Largartón involves a little climb, but there are some great views of Laxe from the top. The end is in sight.

After crossing a stretch of moor-like landscape the path hits a track, turns right and heads along it to visit a particularly dramatic headland, the **Punta Rubia**. After scaring yourself with the views, head west then south with Laxe once again in view. This exposed stretch of coast is much too windy for bracken.

The last stretch of walking is beautiful but takes a long time to complete. There is a hidden cove, **Coído dos Muiños**, with a watermill at its head that has to be walked round before finally starting the home run. Follow a path along a bank squeezed between houses and the sea. The path can be a little overgrown and this only adds to the pleasure of a final walk across a wide beach, the **Praia de Laxe**, into the town from which its name is derived. The stage ends in the little square, Plaza Ramón Juega, next to the hotel/restaurant, the Caso do Arco.

## LAXE

The lovely town of Laxe is dominated by the church of Santa Mariá da Atalaia whose apparent austerity belies its artistic and cultural significance. Parts of the church date from the 14th century but most of it, constructed in Gothic style, was built in the late 15th century. The church has a unique nave with a square apse covered by a classic vaulted Gothic ceiling. The church had an important defensive role overlooking the harbour and was armed with cannon. This enabled defenders to deter intrusion from pirates keen to capture locals and take them into slavery.

Many of the buildings in the town are due to the patronage by the Moscoso family and Doña Urraca de Moscoso in particular. The family came to dominate the local nobility in the 15th century through a process marked by incredible violence where the leadership of women and Doña Urraca de Moscoso in particular played a significant role. The Doña was also responsible for the construction of 'La Casa de Arco', a hostel built to accommodate pilgrims arriving by sea from Ireland, England and France on their way to Santiago de Compostela.

Close to the church, and currently used as a parking place, are the graves of the casualties from the wreck of the Adelaide, which ran aground in rough weather on the beach of Laxe in 1850. The ship, chartered by the British government and on a secret mission to the Caribbean, was carrying weapons, money and a British spy. The only survivor was the captain (who lost his wife and son) and the supposed spy, who was killed after he was discovered in a shed.

Laxe has a choice of places to stay. The Hostal Bahia, which has an exceptionally helpful host, is of particularly good value (www.bahialaxe.com, tel +34 981 728 207). I managed to lose my phone when I staying in Laxe, a potential disaster as it contained my trip notes for this guide, but the manager and his daughter moved heaven and earth to retrieve it. Laxe has two other hotels: the Playa de Laxe (www.playadelaxe.com, tel +34 981 739 000) and the Caso do Arco (www.casadoarco.es, tel +34 981 706 904). It also has several places to eat and if you're still eating fish then try the Mirador, a lively restaurant located south of the main square.

*Heading to the Punta do Cabalo*

# STAGE 4

*Laxe to Arou*

| | |
|---|---|
| **Start** | Plaza Ramón Juega |
| **Finish** | Praia de Arou |
| **Distance** | 18km |
| **Ascent** | 210m |
| **Walking time** | 6hr |

Stage 4 is relatively short with beautiful coastal scenery that is varied and interesting. Highlights include the Praia de Soesto, the salt marches behind the enormous Praia de Traba, the weird rocks near the Punta das Pías, and the museum of the German Hermit at Camelle. It's a lovely walk and, apart from a small climb over the Petón do Castro (rewarded with some of the Camiño's best views), easy.

Waymarking is good and navigation straightforward, although there are tempting wrong turns on the way to Punta das Pías.

For lunch, consider stopping at the café at Mórdomo whose owner is particularly friendly and welcoming to Camiño walkers. There are also plenty of places to eat in Camelle.

## ALTERNATIVE SCHEDULES AND SHORTCUTS

At the time of writing, neither Camelle nor Arou, the two towns close to each other at the end of the route, had any formal accommodation (although Airbnb sometimes comes up with rooms). This may well change in the future and if it does an update will be posted. Without accommodation, you need to organise a taxi back to Laxe and this is best done through the hotel in Laxe. The taxi drivers are used to making the journey and will usually offer a special deal including a return trip next day.

Informal accommodation is apparently available in Arou and, if you're interested, ask for contact details in one of the village's bars (try the Café Bar Galicia). Although this can't be booked in advance, it might be worth a try particularly as there is usually plenty of accommodation in Laxe to fall back on.

From the Plaza Ramón Juega, head north along the main street next to the seafront to the church Igrexa de Santa María da Atalaia. Climb up the steps past the church, turn right into the street above and then, at the next junction, follow signs to the Praia Dos Cristais. Continue to the next junction, following the same signs. At the next junction, bear right and follow the signs to **Faro de Laxe**. Continue to a concrete wall above a quarry then turn left onto a path. Follow this all the way to the lighthouse. It's a stunning path but can be windy.

*With 'A Espera' – the waiting*

The **Faro de Laxe**, another well located lighthouse, is almost identical in shape and size to its cousin across the bay, the Faro do Roncudo. Unlike its cousin however, the Faro de Laxe has a statue – 'A Espera' (the Waiting) – depicting a woman with a baby in her arms, looking worried and staring out to sea hoping for the return of her husband. The last fishing boat to flounder locally was the Playa Armela, which in 1972 hit the rocks immediately west of the peninsula. Eight members of the crew of 10 were lost.

From the statue, follow a path descending across heather in a westerly direction. The path descends to low cliffs and a feature known as the **Furna da Espuma**, a place where the sea hits the cliffs and often generates a foam that looks like snow. Continue south-southeast into a west-facing bay towards a large walled cemetery. Looking west, you can see Camelle and Ajou. Immediately below, on the north side of the cemetery, is the little beach known as the **Praia dos Cristais**.

The small beach north of the cemetery is known as the **Praia dos Cristais**. Originally a dump for bottles, it has now become a local tourist attraction. The heap of broken bottles, battered and polished by the sea, has been turned into a beach of multi-coloured jewels.

Head around the cemetery (you can go either way) and join a path running to the right of a stone wall. After 20m, turn right at a junction and continue on a path above a stony bay (Enseada da Baleeira). The turn at the junction is easily missed.

The next stretch of walking is spectacular with the path sticking close to low, rocky cliffs. The water is so clear that sometimes you can see large fish swimming in the pools below. Looking back into the bay, watch out for caves cut into the cliff face. Follow the path around a small low headland into the next bay. Continue as it starts an ascent through ancient stone-walled fields up the side of the **Petón do Castro**. If you're lucky with the weather, the top is one of best places to be on the whole Camiño.

Descend from the Petón do Castro to the **Praia de Soesto**. The route actually follows duckboards around the back of the bay but a walk across what is an absolutely stunning beach is irresistible – it's the perfect place to be on a breezy day in the sunshine. The path on the other side of the beach is easily found; climb onto it and follow it round a low rocky headland (**Punta Catasol**) to where Camelle once again comes into view. As the path turns south and descends, take the right fork down to the head of a small, probably dry inlet (**Praia do Castrallón**). Turn right above the inlet, follow a path towards the sea and then southwest round the coast to a slightly larger beach (**Praia de Arnado**). Turn right onto a track and follow it for 1km.

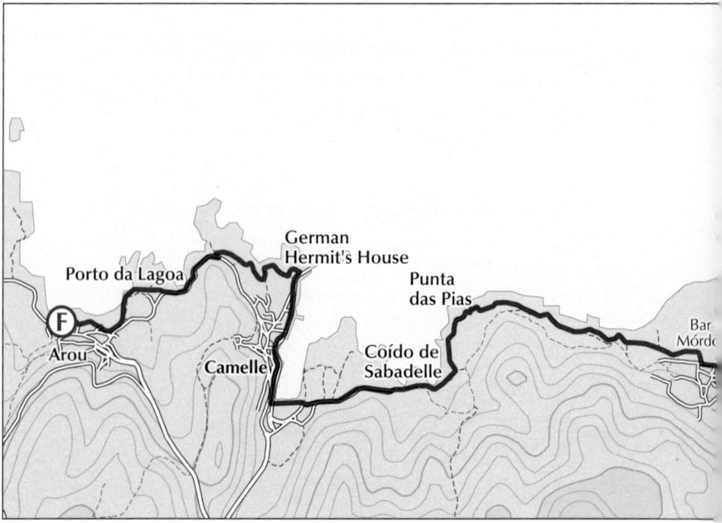

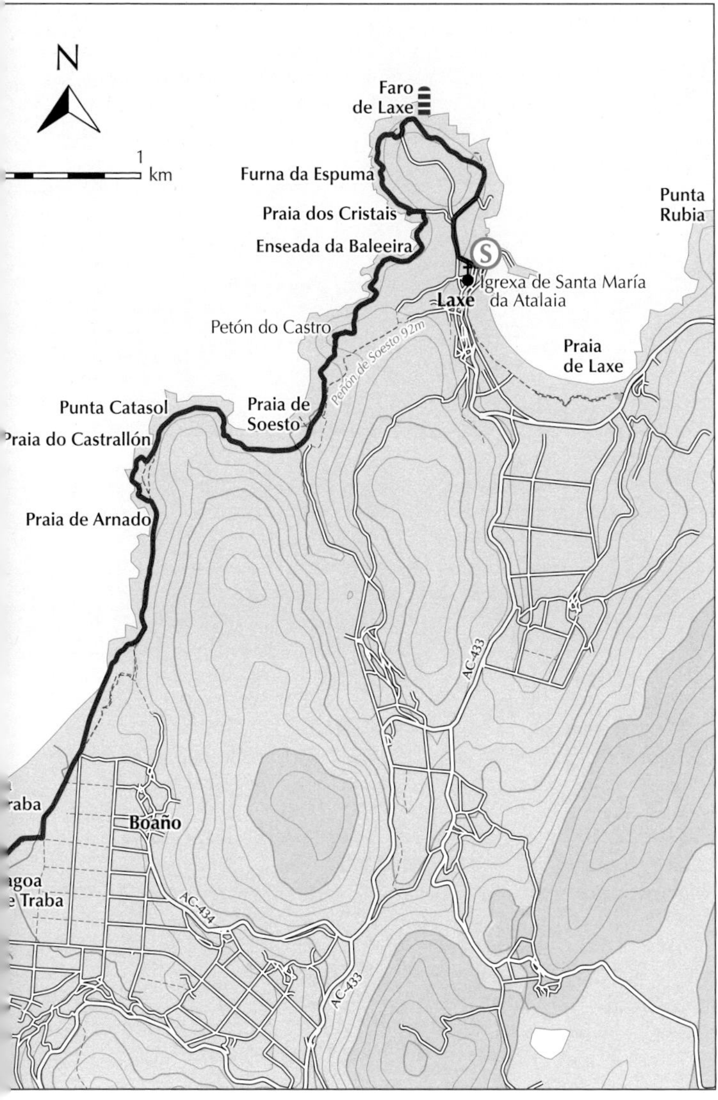
N
1 km
Faro de Laxe
Furna da Espuma
Praia dos Cristais
Enseada da Baleeira
Punta Rubia
S
Igrexa de Santa María da Atalaia
Laxe
Petón do Castro
Peñón de Soesto 92m
Praia de Laxe
Punta Catasol
Praia de Soesto
Praia do Castrallón
Praia de Arnado
AC-433
Boaño
AC-434
AC-433

Continue with the track for 15 minutes, then leave it and take a right-hand turn onto a path. Follow the path through long abandoned walled fields, a little overgrown in places, down towards the sea. At the head of the beach (**Praia de Traba**), which is inland from the village of Boaño, cross a small wooden bridge over a stream onto duckboards. Follow the duckboards to their end and then turn right onto a well-marked path past bird-watching hides through marram grass. The dunes are to the right and a huge area of reeds are to the left – reeds that are hiding the **Lagoa de Traba**, which you get to see for the first time at the last hide. From the hide, follow a gravel track up to a road, turn right and continue for 200m to the **Bar O Mórdomo**, the recommended lunch stop.

From the café, continue along the road and turn right onto duckboards after 100m, going round a play area and out along the coast (ignoring a right hand turn). The duckboards end with a small beach. Cross it and climb onto a path running close to the sea into a landscape made up of small abandoned walled fields and rocky outcrops. The beautifully weathered rocks have a distinct sandy or rusty coloured tinge to them. Watch out for strangely positioned boulders or erratics; there are some great examples here.

Among the boulder field, just beyond a huge slab of rock, take an easily missed right turn off what is a well-defined path. The wrong path takes a more direct route to Camelle but misses what is a magical world of natural boulder sculptures. Eventually the right 'path' disappears altogether and the only means of navigation are markers on the boulders. Following the markers leads you round the **Punta das Pías** with the route turning from westerly to southerly in the process.

The natural boulder sculptures are amazing. Watch out for three huge rocks leaning precariously on each other like drunks – a wild boar pushing a boulder up a hill, and the profile of King Kong.

Emerging from the boulder field, join a more obvious path and follow it through pine trees to join a larger path heading west. Continue as the path turns to a track down to a beach of cobble stones at the head of the **Coído de Sabadelle** and onto a tarmac road. Follow the road for about 700m and, as the road turns left, step down to a muddy beach (Praia de Camelle). Cross the beach, climb steps onto a road and follow it into **Camelle**.

## CAMELLE AND MANFRED GNÄDINGER

Camelle, a port with lots of small bars and restaurants but no accommodation, is famous for two things: its location at the heart of the Costa da Morte, and Manfred Gnädinger, the German Hermit. It's interesting to note that Camelle used to play host to the Barbéito y Cía Salvage Station, a giant scrapyard dedicated to the extraction of metal from shipwrecks.

*Camelle's German*

Manfred Gnädinger's story is a fascinating one. He arrived as a tall, thin, well dressed young man from Germany in 1962, fell in love with a local girl and had his heart broken. He retreated to a hut near the beach, stripped down to a loin cloth and embarked on a life of total self-sufficiency, sustaining himself from the vegetables grown in his tiny garden. Using debris from the sea, he surrounded his hut with sculptures that shared the organic characteristics of Gaudí's work. Although he kept himself to himself, the semi-naked German became popular with the locals who marvelled at his ability to swim in the ocean all year round. In 2002, oil from the Prestige shipwreck destroyed his life's work and a month later he was found dead in his hut. Locals believe that this ecological warrior's death was caused from grief over the oil spill, his second broken heart. The German hermit is regarded as the only human victim of the disaster.

Clearly Camelle remains proud of its German hermit and as well as the hut and sculptures (restored to their original glory), a museum dedicated to his life features in the town centre.

*Wild boar pushing a rock;*

*Huge rock armchair;*

*King Kong?*

Head north through town along the side of the port past the Casa del Alemán (with its statue of the semi-naked German hermit) and a series of small cafés. Next to the main harbour wall immediately north of the town is the **German Hermit's House** surrounded by his artworks. Turn left in front of the house and left again in front of a white house a few metres later. Continue south along a wall path heading back to Camelle and then take a sharp right. Continue on a slightly circuitous route eventually emerging onto the road heading west out of Camelle. Follow the road down a hill and round a small fishing harbour, **Porto da Lagoa**. Turn right onto a path next to the slipway and follow it over a low headland to a pretty little beach, **Praia de Arou**, in front of the town itself.

## NOTE

If you are getting a taxi back to your accommodation from Praia de Arou, you should arrange for the driver to meet you in the car park next to the beach. I'd recommend using Taxi Manolo, tel +34 635 855 723, manutaxilaxe@hotmail.com.

# STAGE 5

*Arou to Camariñas*

| | |
|---|---|
| **Start** | Praia de Arou |
| **Finish** | Porto de Camariñas |
| **Distance** | 23km |
| **Ascent** | 300m |
| **Walking time** | 7hr 40min |

Stage 5 takes the Camiño into the heart of the Costa da Morte. It was shipwrecks along this stretch of coast that earned it its deadly reputation, especially among British sailors. It combines particularly dramatic scenery with some stretches of slightly tedious walking along gravel tracks and roads. The highlights include the climb around the dune near Monte de Veo (the halfway point on the Camiño), the Enseada do Trece bay, the Cemeterio dos Ingleses (The English Cemetery) and the ever changing views of the most stunning of all Camiño lighthouses, the Faro do Cabo Vilán. Although views of the lighthouse are a major compensation, the road walking involved in getting to it is tedious.

Apart from the café at the Faro do Cabo Vilán there is nowhere en route for lunch, so consider packing a picnic.

## ALTERNATIVE SCHEDULES AND SHORTCUTS

By applying a little surgery to the route to the north and west of Camariñas, the day can be made shorter.

The first adaptation involves missing the visit to the lighthouse. It includes some of the road walking but cuts off the peninsula to the south of a huge ugly fish farm, rejoining the track on the west facing coast. This reduces the walk by 4km and saves an hour.

The second adjustment involves missing the visit to Ermita de Nosa Señora do Montea and, instead of sticking to the coastline, taking a more direct route into Camariñas. This would save 3km and 40 minutes.

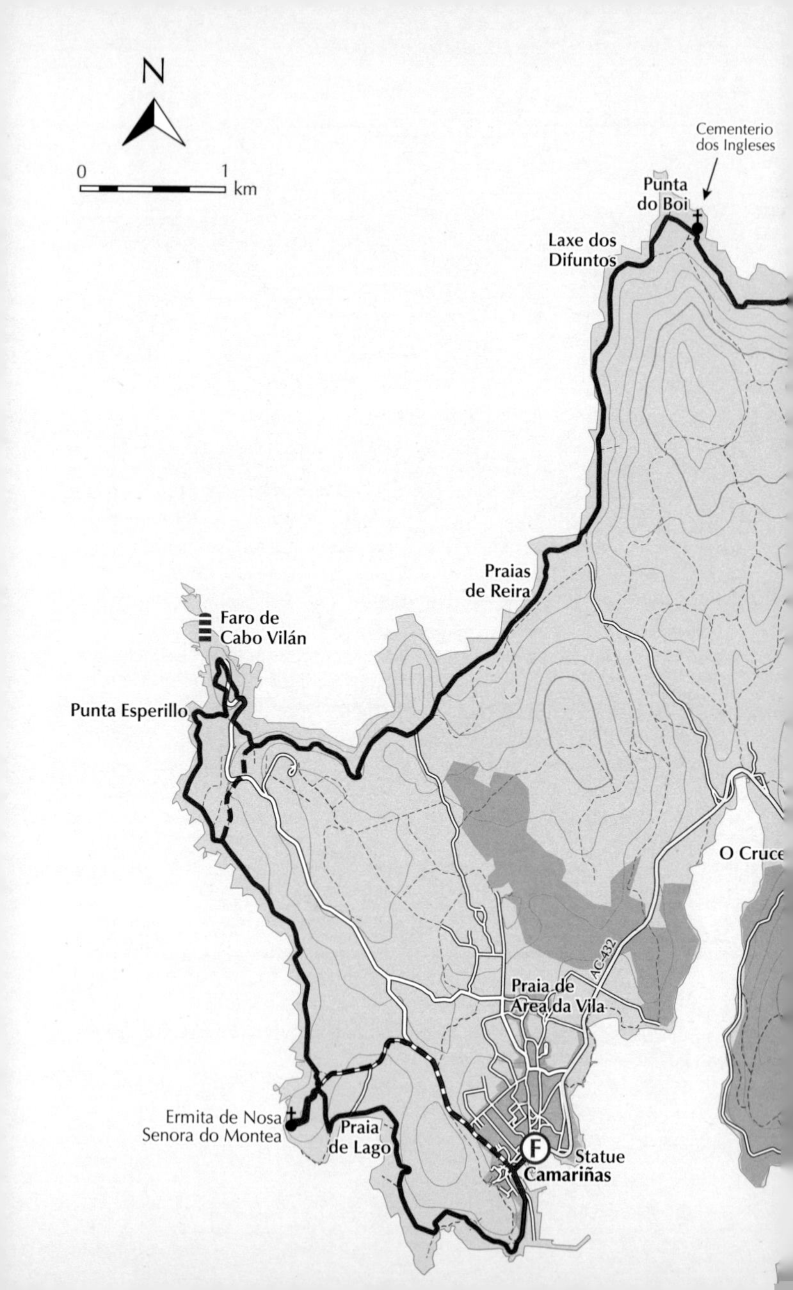
N
0
1
km
Cementerio
dos Ingleses
Punta
do Boi
Laxe dos
Difuntos
Praias
de Reira
Faro de
Cabo Vilán
Punta Esperillo
O Cruce
AC-432
Praia de
Area da Vila
Ermita de Nosa
Senora do Montea
Praia
de Lago
F
Statue
Camariñas

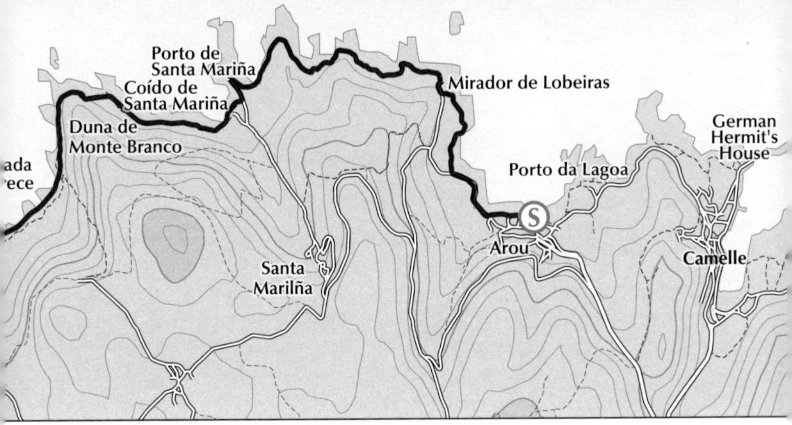


From the **Praia de Arou**, join the path heading west round the beach to duckboards. Continue along the duckboards to a track and follow it to a road. After 300m leave the road as it starts to climb and join a path on the right. Follow it through abandoned walled fields close to the seashore. Just before the headland turn left and follow the path on short climb up to a small car park and viewing point, Mirador de Lobeiras.

Follow the road down to beach, the Praia de Lobeiras, and join a path just in front of low fishing shacks. After a brief but energy-sapping sandy stretch follow an easier path through beds of heather. Continue with the path, which involves occasional short stretches of boulder hopping, for just over a kilometre. After crossing a low headland, **Porto de Santa Mariña**, an uninhabited fishing harbour comes into view.

From the headland follow the path through stacks of crabbing pots to the white buildings of the little harbour. To find the path out, join the road on the other side of the buildings and follow it inland. Turn right onto a track that turns into a path. The path is to the left of a couple of grey buildings set off from the road.

## COSTA DA MORTE

The website www.wrecksite.eu aggregates charts from around the world and pinpoints known shipwrecks. The coastline of northwest Spain as a whole is over-represented but the stretch that has by far the highest density of shipwrecks is the north-facing coast from just east of Camelle through to the Cabo Vilán. As well as storms that typically affect the whole coast, this is an area where ships change direction and where just a marginal miscalculation can lead them onto the numerous reefs that lie just below the water surface.

The source of the term 'Costa da Morte' is unknown but its use became widespread among British sailors following extreme loss of life in a series of disasters in the late 19th century. These disasters prompted the British to press for improved maritime signalling and resulted in the inauguration of the Faro de Cabo Vilán in 1896.

Particularly offensive to local historians are accusations of 'land piracy'. Coastal communities in Western Europe are routinely accused of placing torches on the horns of cows to confuse navigators on ships. Although the cargo from wrecks was looted by locals there is no documentary evidence that they engaged in practices leading to shipwrecks. Instead, there are plenty of examples of locals risking their own lives to save victims of some of the most treacherous seas in the world.

Head down to a pebbly cove, the **Coído de Santa Mariña**, full of washed up detritus, and join a path on the other side. Take a grassy flower filled path (honeysuckle in July) and embark on what is perhaps the toughest climb of the Camiño,

*Thankfully beached on the Praia Lobeiras*

around the **Duna de Monte Branco**. There are bigger climbs but the sandy path is energy-sapping. The vegetation is particularly delicate on the dune and, to preserve it, the route has been diverted since my last trip; instead of crossing the saddle and the dune, pass to the right of the little summit on the seaward side.

The **Duna de Monte Branco**, a pass on the way to the wild beaches between the Cabo Veo and the Cabo do Trece, is the highest sand dune in Spain. The local ecosystem is very delicate. Among the flora is a shrub known as the *caramiña*, which can grow in extremely severe weather conditions and which is now endangered and almost unique to this area. The village of Camariñas was named after it.

Once you get to the top, the views across the bay, **Enseada do Trece**, are wonderful but if it's windy the sand blast calls for a quick descent. On my last visit the weather was perfect and a strong onshore wind was so powerful that even the white horses had their heads down. The tops of the waves, across a stunning aquamarine sea, were sheared off by the wind and sent away in huge clouds of misty spray. I felt lucky to be there.

*Crossing the Praia do Treco*

## THE DREADFUL 1890s

Between 1875 and 1940, at least 49 ships floundered on rocks between Cabo Vilán and Camelle but it was a series of disasters in the 1890s (13 ships lost in that decade alone) that established the reputation of the Costa da Morte and prompted the authorities to act.

Three of the 10 ships suffered a significant loss of life. All three were sailing under a British flag, and the details of what happened have been recorded.

The first, and for the British Navy the most embarrassing, was the loss of HMS Serpent. Only launched in 1887, this was a modern torpedo cruiser, 75m long with 175 crew members, and fitted with the latest equipment. Despite an experienced crew, faulty navigation in a strong southwesterly gale led the ship onto the rocks near Punta do Boi. The stranded ship survived on the rocks for less than an hour, and with huge waves breaking over it, successive efforts to launch the ship's lifeboats proved futile. It must have been desperate although contemporary reports maintain that discipline was sustained to the end when all but three of the crew perished. The three survivors had one thing in common – they all wore life jackets. It was because of the loss of the HMS Serpent that, for the first time, life jackets became compulsory throughout the British Navy.

Three years later, the SS Trinacria, a cargo ship propelled by steam and sail and on its way to Naples with a crew of 37 and four passengers (four Methodist missionaries), found itself too close to the Cabo Vilán. Its captain took evasive action too late and at six in the morning it hit rocks immediately west of the Punta do Boi near the Enseada de Lucin. Seven of the crew managed to make it ashore with the rest perishing on board. The hull of the ship broke up over the next few days; logs, ropes, and wax, combined with the bodies of the dead, were deposited on the beach. Unable to identify the victims and to prevent further decomposition, the locals constructed a funeral pyre and the bodies were burnt. The little beach near the site is known as the 'A Playa da Furna dos Difuntos' – the beach where bodies were burnt.

After the Serpent and Trinacria the decision was taken to build the Faro do Cabo Vilán, but it didn't prevent the third major disaster of the 1890s.The loss of the City of Agra in 1897 was subject to a Board of Trade enquiry, the report of which is fascinating as it brings to life the experience of a ship hitting the rocks. The City of Agra, another modern ship, had left Liverpool heading for Calcutta with 3,500 tons of cargo, 71 crew, two passengers and two stowaways. It had lifeboats and life jackets for 140. Most of the crew were Indians. Steaming southwest into the teeth of a winter storm, the second officer – on watch – suddenly sees waves breaking close on the starboard side. He orders the ship to steer astern but it's too late, and with a great crash the ship hits the rocks. The enquiry report provides graphic detail of the efforts made to launch the ship's four lifeboats amid the storm and a panicking crew. Stranded on the rocks, the vessel, more than 100m long, lasts for less than 12 minutes. Rather than being launched, the lifeboats were washed off the ship's deck. The stowaways – hiding in the boats – were particularly fortunate but somehow 42 people made it to the lifeboats or survived clinging onto wreckage. Some were saved by the inhabitants of Camelle and Arou and some were saved the next day by another British ship. The bravery of the locals who participated in the rescue was recognised by the British government and the boat bell was given as a present to the church of Espíritu Santo in Camelle.

Another navigational error was the ultimate cause of the disaster and, although the lighthouse was now up and working, the watch didn't see the light.

Descend carefully down towards the bay following a well-defined track. Make your way across a series of four beaches each separated by rocks. A gap in the rocks at the side of the fourth beach welcomes you back to a path. Follow the path across a wide grassy bank onto cobbles. Cross the cobbles and take the path through low prickly bushes into a wider path. In April, I found this wider path full of water and, with prickly bushes on either side, wading was the only option.

The **Cemeterio dos Ingleses** (the English Cemetery) was the burial place for those who perished following the loss of the SS Iris in 1883 (when 35 people drowned). Located immediately to the east of Cabo Veo, it was extended to accommodate the graves of the sailors who lost their lives on the HMS Serpent in 1890.

*Dozens of little cairns near the Cemeterio dos Ingleses*

*Faro do Cabo Vilán*

Stay on a path to the seaward side of the Cementerio dos Ingleses and, after passing hundreds of little cairns, head northwest towards the headland, the **Punta do Boi**. Just before the headland, look west to see for first time the Camiño's most dramatically located lighthouse, Faro do Cabo Vilán. From the low headland join a dirt road and follow it south for 2km, passing a row of houses and a large anchor on the side of the road. At the brow of a low hill, leave the road and turn right onto a sandy path. Turn right again after a few metres and cross a small beach (Praias de Reira). Follow a path over a low grassy headland, with views of the lighthouse improving all the time, past duckboards, and around the Praia da Balea, a beach that attracts windsurfers.

After crossing another headland drop down to a small beach, cross it, and join a path that takes you to some duckboards. Turn right at the end of the duckboards, right again and follow a path heading up to the ridge on the left. It's quite a stiff climb and takes you, near the top, back onto the dirt road. Just around the corner (the summit at the end of the ridge is A Pedrosa) is a car park with amazing views of the **Faro do Cabo Vilán**. From here, it's 2km to the lighthouse. The route mostly follows the road but shortens the journey somewhat by cutting across two of the switchbacks.

### First shortcut

If taking the first shortcut, don't leave the road to join the path at the first switchback. Instead, follow the road south and leave it to join a track on the left just it completes its first switchback. From the track head southwest down to the sea and join the main route running south parallel with the coast.

From the car park head up to the old lighthouse. From the here you should see Muxia; it looks a long way away but it's tomorrow's target.

## FARO DE CABO VILÁN

Located at the end of a promontory on 100m high cliffs, the Faro de Cabo Vilán enjoys a dramatic location. The lighthouse, built as a result of the loss of life in the 1890s, is the oldest electric lighthouse in Spain and the only one on the Camiño dos Faros that is still occupied. The light from the tower can be seen 28 miles away, and when it was built it was one of the most powerful lights in the world. In 1933, the building was declared a national monument. It includes a museum, which houses some of the older optics and other devices related to the history of the lighthouse; a centre for the study of the wrecks; an exhibition room; and a café.

On the high ground immediately south of the lighthouse is an octagonal tower which, from 1854, was the location of a steam-driven lighthouse. The choice of location proved to be a poor one and from certain angles rocks obscured the view of the light for sailors at sea. Despite efforts to dynamite the rocks, this problem was never resolved.

The fish farm immediately south of the Cabo Vilán produces turbot. It is one of the largest farms of its type in the world, and part of what is a very significant local fish farming industry.

From the old lighthouse, follow a path through heather and gorse along a circuitous route back to the road. Walk down the road for a few metres then take a right turn onto a path heading down the side of the fish farm (more industrial complex than farm). As the path nears the sea, turn left around some outlet pipes (near **Punta Esperillo**) and join a track going south on the seaward side of the fish farm.

After navigating an unpleasant stretch of walking and getting past the fish farm things improve. The next target, the Ermita de Nosa Señora do Montea (a chapel on top of a headland directly south), should be visible and the track to get to it is etched into sloping hillside running down to a rocky coast. Stay on the track – navigation for the next 2km is straightforward. Continue to a junction (there is a football pitch behind a fence on the left) and turn right. After a few metres, turn right again and follow the track up to the **Ermita de Nosa Señora do Montea**. Return to the same point once the visit has been completed. The church was built in the 18th century on the site of an older one and is a great place to enjoy the sunset.

### Second shortcut

To start the second shortcut, turn left instead of right at the first junction and follow the road past the playing field east and south into Camariñas. It's about 2km from the turn-off to the harbour and accommodation.

Go south from the junction and follow a track through pine trees. Continue as it swings sharply left and head down to the beach (the **Praia de Lago**). Follow the track around the beach and back into pine trees. Watch out for the trawler that has somehow found itself several hundred metres inland.

Continue on the track past a small holding. Turning right, leave the pine trees and head back to the coast. Follow the walled track around a low headland, leave it and join a path going east across the end of a cove. Back at the track, turn right and right again near a garden wall. Turn left at a junction with a road and take the next right into **Porto de Camariñas**.

## CAMARIÑAS

Camariñas is largest town on the Camiño dos Faros and has a population of just over 6000. Built around a lovely port, it is important for fishing, fish farming and fish canning.

In addition to fish, Camariñas is also famous for bobbin lacemaking (*pallilear*), a tradition imported via trade with ports in Flanders in the 16th century. At its height, some 2000 women were involved in lace-making, and products were exported around the world, particularly to the Americas.

The town has a particularly big festival in mid July, which should be either embraced or avoided, depending on your preference for crowds.

There are four hotels in Camariñas, none of which are particularly special. The best located are the Hotel Puerto Arnela (www.hotelpuertoarnela.com, tel +34 981 737 240) and the Hotel O Paranda (www.oparranda.com, tel +34 677 433 303), although the Pensión Gaviota (tel +34 981 736 326) is not far from the seafront. The Stella del Mar is located away from seafront (+34 981 737 304).

*The harbour at Camariñas*

# STAGE 6

*Camariñas to Muxía*

| | |
|---|---|
| **Start** | Porto de Camariñas |
| **Finish** | Porto de Muxía |
| **Distance** | 29.5km |
| **Ascent** | 470m |
| **Walking time** | 8hr 40min |

Like Stage 2, Stage 6 involves going inland to cross a river. It's a long stage, and although the walking is easy and nearly always flat, getting all the way from Camariñas to Muxia in a single day is tough and involves either an early start or a late finish. While never dull, Stage 6 is the Camiño's least interesting stage and there isn't time in the walking schedule to spend time exploring the main attraction, the church, castle and tidal mill at Cereixo. Completing the whole stage in a day is feasible but most people will want to consider alternative schedules or shortcuts, and plenty of options are available.

To get Muxia from Camariñas you have to cross a bridge over the river, Rio do Porto, at Ponte do Porte. Getting to the bridge involves a meandering walk east around a ria. Most of the walking is in trees close to the water and, with constantly changing views, it is very pleasant. The final stretch, however, where the route visits a series of little villages on the approach to Ponte do Porte, is not so attractive.

From Ponte do Porte to Muxia, the route also has its good and not-so-good parts. After Cereixo, the route heads west along the south shore of the estuary and visits the little beach resort at Praia do Lago before embarking on a short but annoying stretch of road walking. Fortunately normal service is soon resumed with the route returning to the coast along another little valley packed with ancient watermills.

The route is generally easy to follow – but beware of taking a wrong turn in the little villages before Ponte do Porte.

There are plenty of places to stop for lunch but the café and restaurant at Ponte do Porte are particularly well positioned.

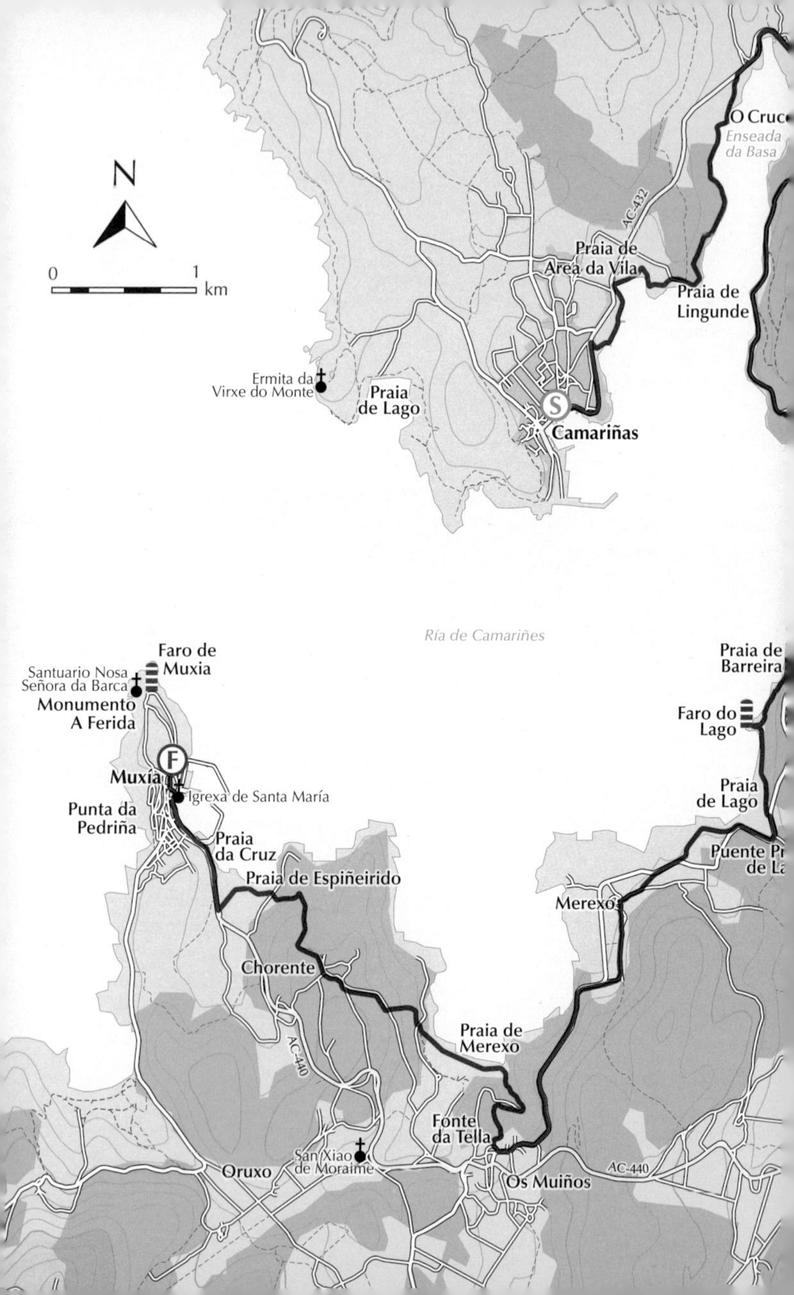

N
0
1
km
O Cruc
Enseada da Basa
AC-432
Praia de Area da Vila
Praia de Lingunde
Ermita da Virxe do Monte
Praia de Lago
S
Camariñas
Ría de Camariñes
Faro de Muxia
Santuario Nosa Señora da Barca
Monumento A Ferida
F
Muxía
Igrexa de Santa María
Punta da Pedriña
Praia da Cruz
Praia de Espiñeirido
Chorente
AC-440
Praia de Merexo
Fonte da Tella
San Xiao de Moraime
Oruxo
Os Muiños
Merexo
Praia de Barreira
Faro do Lago
Praia de Lago
Puente Pr de La

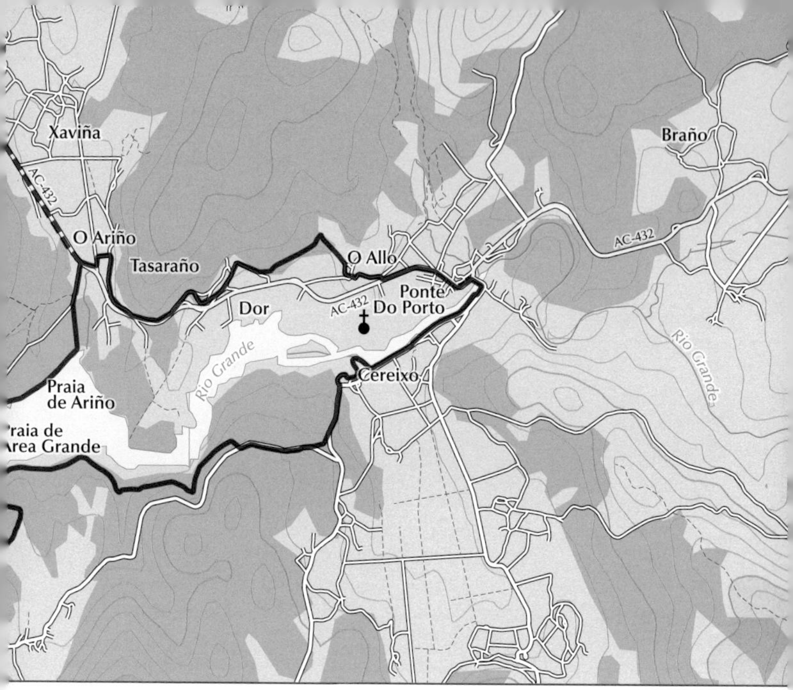


## ALTERNATIVE SCHEDULE AND SHORTCUTS

The simplest approach for walkers who want to complete the Camiño but don't want to walk the whole of Stage 6 in one day is to split it in two and stay overnight in Ponte do Porte. This adds an extra day to the overall schedule but removes the time pressure. In addition to Ponte do Porte, there are other accommodation options. If you'd prefer beachside accommodation, try the Hostal Playa de Lago, which is another 8km along the route.

If it is not possible for you to add an extra day to your schedule, then consider taking a taxi either to Ponte do Porto or from Ponte do Porto to Muxia. Both halves of the stage have their strengths and weaknesses but if forced to choose I would miss the first half, taxi to Ponte de Porto, and spend a bit of time visiting the sites at Cereixo.

There is one simple shortcut that can be fed into the Stage 6 route planning mix and this involves not going round peninsula, the Enseada da Basa, which separates the bay from the river estuary, the Ría do Porto. Joining the route involves a short road walk but it reduces the walk length by 4km.

Working on a boat near Camariñas

From the harbour, walk along the seafront and follow the main road north past a statue on a plinth. Take a right turn just before the Group Cerdeimar fish canning factory and head down to the sea. Take the promenade to the beach, **Praia de Area da Vila**, go down the steps and walk across the beach to the southeast corner, before scrambling up a path and turning right onto the track above. Follow the track (which turns into a road at one point) south through pine, eucalyptus and oak. Go past a lovely beach, the **Praia de Ligunde**, before turning east into a bay, the **Enseada da Basa**.

The **Enseada da Basa** and the estuary to the south, Río do Porto, are particularly rich in shellfish. The carefully managed industry, which produces clams, cockles, and razor clams, is an important activity for local people.

In the summer months, expect to see seaweed drying. It is used as a source of carrageenan, a food additive.

Follow a lovely grassy track east into the bay for 800m where it ends at the shoreline. Continue along rocks for a few metres thankfully turning inland to join a path. After 200m the path, which could be a little overgrown, emerges near a small inlet after which it joins a track. After crossing through a more open scrubby landscape, join main road, the **AC-432**. Follow this road, which can be busy, round the head of bay, over the bridge and up to **O Cruceiro**. The rocks just offshore here are a favourite spot for herons. For the shortcut, continue along the main road over the top of the hill and down to the roadside bar, the O Ariño, to rejoin the main route.

At the top of the hill in O Cruceiro, take a right hand turn (there is a hórreo on the left). Follow a small road downhill and take a left hand turn at a fork. Follow this road down to the bay and continue along what is now a wide gravel track around its south side. As the track turns south, after around 2.4km, turn right onto a grassy track taking a left hand turn onto a path shortly after. Head down to a small and very lovely beach and continue along a path round the headland. Stick close to the shoreline (now in the estuary, the Ría do Porto) and after passing picnic tables, walk along the beach, **Praia de Ariño**, which is hard work in the soft sand. After 300m leave the beach taking a path through trees. As the estuary narrows the path turns to a track, then joins a tarmac road (the one that goes to the picnic tables) going east back to the main road. The bay here provides some of the best shellfish in Galicia.

Cross the main road, pass the **O Ariño** restaurant on the left and take the first right along a small road up into **Tasaraño**. At the top of the road, turn right onto a concrete road. After a few metres there is a fountain, which is good for drinking water. Continue along the concrete road, ignoring a turn to the right, all the way to the main road. Immediately to the left is a track. Follow it for 300m turning left at a junction with a small road. In another 100m, turn right. Follow the road through the village of **Dor**, taking care to ignore the first left and taking the second left on a road through the lower old part of village.

Continue on the road out the village then turn left onto a forest track. After 100m, take a right-hand fork onto another track and follow it for 400m to a road into the village of **O Allo**. Continue through the village past some fairly basic play equipment and out to the next village of Collegio. Turn right in the centre of this village onto the main road and follow it into **Ponte do Porto**.

*A Ponto do Porto*

## PONTO DO PORTO AND CEREIXO

Ponto do Porto, built around an elegant medieval bridge, and Cereixo almost join up and it's Cereixo that has the most interesting buildings. The town dates back to before the 10th century but after being destroyed by successive Viking raids was given a new lease of life when King Alfonso XII gave it a town charter enabling the construction of defensive walls and a port. The Romanesque church, Igrexa de Santiago de Cereixo, is the oldest building and dates from the mid 12th century. A typanum on a side door depicts the earliest representation of the transfer of the body to St James to Galicia. The towers, Torres-Pazo de Cereixo, were built in the 16th century and the innovative tidal mill was built in the 17th century.

For accommodation in Ponto do Porto try Hostal O Pincho (tel +34 981 730 250).

*Igrexa de Santiago de Cereixo*

Follow the main road to the bridge, cross it and head west along the river on the other side. After nearly 1km, turn right and join a track running between the river and huge ancient walls of **Cereixo**. Go through the site up to the twin towers then follow the old road back down to the main road and turn right. Go up the main road and, just after the cemetery, Cementerio de Cereixo, take a right-hand turn onto a path to another road. Follow the road west for 100m and then right onto a lovely forest path that heads down to the river. Continue with the path as it crosses a little valley onto a track on the other side. Follow this

for 400m eventually returning to the side of the estuary, **Praia de Area Grande**. After another 800m the route turns inland along a path. As it turns south west, it joins a track. Follow this track for 800m (ignoring turns off) to a junction with a country road.

At a junction turn right downhill (the road turns to a track) past a campsite on the left and down to a beach, **Praia da Barreira**. Around two-thirds of the way across the beach, find a path that climbs into trees and swings west. Follow this increasingly rocky path for 500m emerging onto a small rocky promontory, Punta do Lago, featuring an equally small lighthouse. From the lighthouse, cross the beach (**Praia do Lago**), aiming for a point near the end of the trees. Head through car parks to the road and turn right.

There is summer-only accommodation at the Hostal Praia do Lago (www.hotelplayadelago.com, +34 981 750 793).

From the car park, take the road over a bridge, **Puente Praia de Lago**, and up a hill. As the road starts to turn a corner join a path on the right along a cliff-top path through trees (ignoring several paths to the left). Turn right onto a road and take this for 200m before turning left onto a path into the little village of **Merexo**. Joining a road turn right, and shortly after, in the village centre, turn left. Continue up the hill leaving the village and after 300m turn right onto a larger road. Follow this road all the way to **Os Muiños**.

The fact that this stretch of road walking is shared with a stretch of the Camiño de Santiago doesn't make it any better. Unlike 'pelegrinos', we 'tranos' are not used to road walking and expect better things. In Os Muinos, turn right at a sign pointing to the Fonts da Tella and, ignoring the Camiño signs behind, turn right again. Unlike the 'Camiño' we're taking the scenic route and heading down a lovely valley, the Paseo do Río Negro (molinos). After a few metres on a concrete road, take the stairs down to an old communal washing area – **Fonte da Tella**. Continue along a shaded path, mainly on duckboards, past a series of mills. Ignore signs to the left just after the duckboards and continue down to the beach, **Praia de Merexo**. Go right across the beach and follow a steep path up to a road. Cross the road to a path on the left and go up, heading into eucalyptus trees. Follow the path left along a steep sandy climb, turning right onto a road before the top. Continue along the road, take a right turn at a junction and, after a left turn at a fork, go through the little village of **Chorente**. Bear right at the edge of the village (now back on the Camiño) and enjoy views across the bay.

As the road finishes, join a grassy track heading down through pine trees. Continue for 200m with Muxia coming into view as the trees finish. After crossing a small road, join duckboards in front of the beach, **Praia de Espiñeirido**, and follow them to another beach, **Praia da Cruz**. The main road into **Muxia** is on the other side of this beach and, depending on conditions, either cross it or walk around it.

*Approaching the Praia de Merexo*

## MUXIA

Muxia has become an alternative destination to Fisterra for pelegrinos completing their walk along the St James Way, encouraged perhaps by the version of the St James story that has his body arriving here and drifting on a boat, after he was beheaded in Rome. To get to Muxia they will have left the Camiño main route some 30km before its end and turned northwest. From Muxia another route then heads south, just inland from the coast, to Fisterra. Already a nice town, the influx of pilgrims has added significantly to Muxia's prosperity and a wide range of accommodation is available.

There are two significant Romanesque buildings: the Santuario de Nosa Señora da Barca, a church to the north of the town (most of the surviving building is early 18th century), dramatically located at the end of the promontory; and the San Xiao de Moraime, a monastery about 3km to the south. The monastery is particularly important and significant in the conversion of this part of Spain to Christianity, which came late. Unfortunately, unlike the church, the monastery is not directly on the route and unless you're particularly interested it will be missed.

Unmissable is the memorial to the Prestige oil disaster, a great slab of stone with a huge gash through it symbolising a wound.

Muxia has a good selection of accommodation including Hotel de Encanto A de Loló (www.adelolo.com, tel +34 981 742 422), Hostal de la Cruz (www.hostal-lacruz.com, tel +34 981 742 084) and the Hábitat Cm Muxia (tel +34 981 742 148). There is a parador being built to the west of the town, the Parador Muxia, above the Praia de Lourido and this will presumably be taking bookings at some point from 2020 onwards.

# STAGE 7

*Muxía to Praia de Nemiña*

| | |
|---|---|
| **Start** | Tourist information office, Muxía |
| **Finish** | Praia de Nemiña |
| **Distance** | 26.5km |
| **Ascent** | 910m |
| **Walking time** | 7hr 25min |

After a gentle Stage 6, full blooded coastal walking returns for the last two stages with Stage 7 arguably the toughest day of the whole Camiño and perhaps the most beautiful.

This is the hilliest stage and involves climbing over three mini-summits, Monte Cachelmo (174m), Monte Buitra (164m), and Monte do Pedrouzo (272m). Although none of these climbs are difficult the long walk up Monte do Pedrouzo seems to take forever, particularly if the weather is not friendly.

The stage also rounds three peninsulas, the Punta da Barca, immediately to the north of Muxia, Punta da Buitra and the Cabo Touriñán. While all the walking is excellent, the stretch along the west-facing flank of the second peninsula, a contouring path high above a huge bay (Enseada de Cuína), is particularly good.

There is of course a lot to see in Muxia, in particular the Sanctuary of Nosa Señora da Barca, the lighthouse and the memorial to the Prestige oil disaster. An early decision, discussed below, is whether to try and visit these sights at the end of Stage 6 or the start of Stage 7.

This stage is also remote. The countryside is empty, and indeed there is nowhere on the route to stop for lunch, so a picnic is an essential requirement.

From the tourist information office one street back from the port, head north. After 200m, climb the steps running parallel with street up to a little church, **Igrexa de Santa María**, turn left and climb steps to the right of a belfry. Join a path taking a steep climb to the top of Monte do Corpiño (68m). From the summit follow a paved path down to the church, **Santuario Nosa Señora da Barca** and down to the lighthouse, **Faro de Muxia**. Return to the church and the **Monumento A Ferida**. A Camiño sign says that it's 31km to Fisterra.

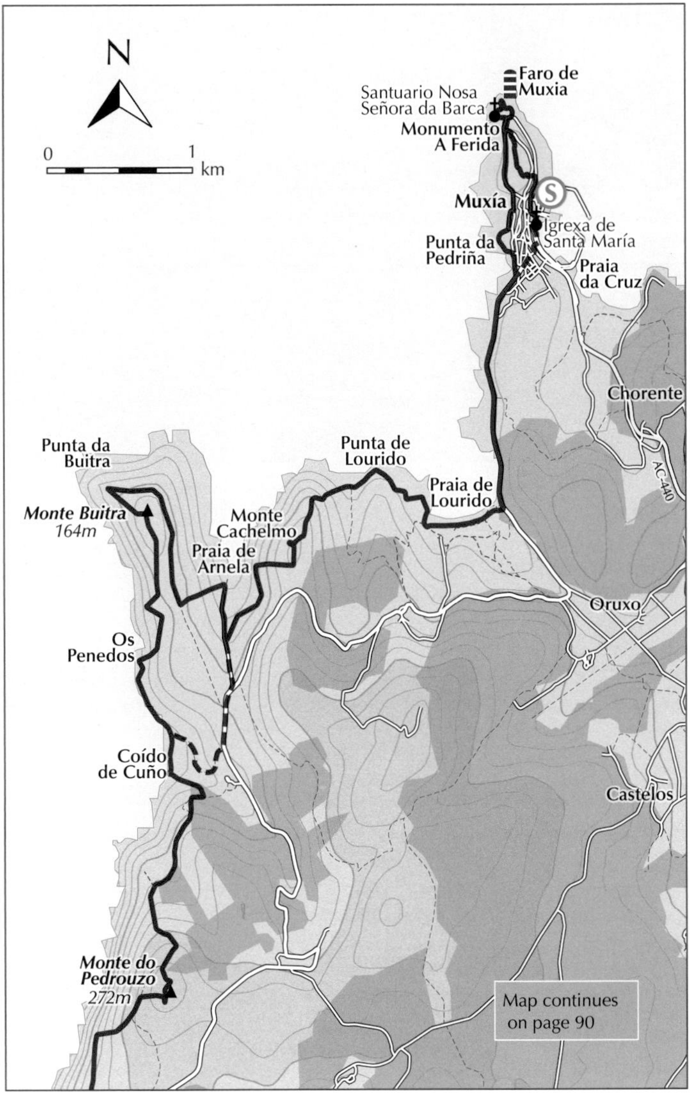
N
0
1
km
Faro de Muxia
Santuario Nosa Señora da Barca
Monumento A Ferida
Muxía
Igrexa de Santa María
Punta da Pedriña
Praia da Cruz
Chorente
AC-440
Punta da Buitra
Punta de Lourido
Praia de Lourido
Monte Buitra
164m
Monte Cachelmo
Praia de Arnela
Oruxo
Os Penedos
Coído de Cuño
Castelos
Monte do Pedrouzo
272m
Map continues on page 90

*Santuario de Nosa Señora da Barca*

From the church head south back into town. Bear right at the Rúa Pedriña and then left again and continue down the hill to a gravel road. Join a path to the right of a low white building and continue on a coastal path round a small headland, **Punta da Pedriña**, and back to an esplanade. From the esplanade join the main road south and follow it for about 1.8km. Leave the road at the bottom of the hill and follow a path that starts at the end of the crash barrier down to the beach, **Praia de Lourido**. Aim for the low white building and head across the sand. Join a path just in front of the building and turn right. Follow the track up the hill and as it turns join a path on the seaward edge of a field. Continue on this path around the headland.

## PARADOR DE MUXIA

Sitting above the Praia de Lourido is the Parador de Muxia. The new hotel should be nearer completion by the time this guide has been published but building has been held up for some time by Spain's financial crisis and changes in government, both regionally and nationally. Paradors are state-owned hotels and technically this is a public building. With a budget of €127million, this is by far the largest one on the Costa da Morte. Its construction apparently dates back to promises made after the Prestige oil disaster and, although the desire to bring jobs to the area can be understood, the building seems totally out of scale for its location.

Ancient fields on the side of Cachelmo

After rounding the first headland and crossing a cove, follow a steep path up the first of the day's 'big' climbs, Monte Cachelmo. From the top of Monte Cachelmo, enjoy the views back to Muxia.

Follow a path initially heading south. From the top it's easy to miss this path so if you're not confident that you're on it go back and start again. After around 200m, turn west onto a broader path bordered by gorse and start a steep descent. The path emerges onto a track and the route heads inland to a junction at the bottom of a valley. At the junction, turn right and follow a track towards the beach, **Praia de Arnela**. After passing between gates, take a sharp left and follow an unpleasant path up the side of a valley between rows of trees in a conifer plantation.

**Second shortcut option**

If the second of the three shortcut options is being taken, turn left instead of right at the junction. After 300m turn left onto a road and follow it south for another 400m and turn right onto a track just after the roadside 12km marker. Follow the track on a meandering descent down to the coast and back to the Camiño.This will save you 90min.

Emerging from the conifers, turn right and follow a gently climbing track north. At the end of the track (and the end of the **Punta da Buitra**), join a path heading south and make the short climb to the top of **Monte Buitra**. From the top, continue south along a narrow scratchy path descending gently through gorse. After turning west and making a steeper descent, turn left onto a track and follow it uphill for about 200m to a junction with a path. Turn right onto the path and follow it down through a struggling conifer plantation to the little spit, the **Os Penedos**. The views of the cliffs to the west and north are particularly dramatic. If it's not too windy consider stopping here to eat a picnic.

From Os Penedos continue along a classic coastal path for 500m, down to meadows (**Coído de Cuño**). Head across the meadows following the coast. If you have taken the second shortcut option, rejoin the main route here. Cross the stream at the other side of the second meadow, and follow a path running inland and parallel with the stream. Ignore the path immediately to the right. The correct path, which could be overgrown, takes you through a grove of stumpy oaks.

After following the stream for nearly 300m, the path turns right and climbs steeply into pine trees. An easier path then takes you across a shallow valley, crossing a junction with a track on the way up the other side. From the junction, start a steady and relentless climb to the top of Monte do Pedrouzo. The summit is marked by a pile of huge boulders that appear to have been dumped in the middle of a meadow.

At the top of **Monte do Pedrouzo**, enjoy the view of Cabo Touriñán.

From the summit, follow a well-defined, easy-to-follow path heading northwest (towards the end of the peninsula) down to a track and continue for 600m. Turn right onto another well-trodden path and take it all the way down to the **Praia de Moreira**.

After crossing a small stream, follow the track on the other side of the beach over a low headland. About 100m after crossing a junction with another track south, turn south towards pine trees and a rocky outcrop. Continue on this track, which gets progressively larger, and, ignoring a sharp turn to the right, continue towards the houses in the hills above. About 100m before the first house, take a right onto a similar track. Ignoring turns to the right and left, follow this track for around 1km to a crossroads at the bottom of a hill and turn right. Continue north for 100m turning left into a lovely sunken lane (flooded early in the season) which, ignoring turn offs, can be followed west all the way to the junction with the road to **Touriñán**. The junction is the point at which the third shortcut option kicks in, saving you 90min. If the option is taken, turn left here rather than right.

The lighthouse, **Faro Touriñán**, was built in 1981 to replace the one constructed in 1898, at the same time as Faro Vilán. Interestingly, the 1898 lighthouse used the optics from the original Faro Vilán, the one built in the 1850s, and had a range of 10 miles. The current lighthouse has a range of 23.

## THE SINKING OF THE PRESTIGE

The memorial to the Prestige oil disaster

The sinking of the Prestige oil tanker in 2002 was Spain's worst ever ecological disaster and a terrible story of buck passing and incompetence. Hitting November storms, the ship, a single hulled oil tanker, Greek operated, Liberian registered, carrying 77,000 tons of fuel oil, which had been poorly inspected in Russia and probably shouldn't have been at sea, started to take on water 50km off the coast of Finisterre.

Controversy and litigation surround the subsequent decisions but the captain's request to dock the ship was refused by the Spanish government with the French and Portuguese governments also insisting that it kept out of their coastal waters. Six days later, and after being dragged further into international waters, the ship sank. Instead of freezing in the ship as hoped, a huge quantity of oil was released hitting the coast of Galicia in particular but also the rest of the coast of northern Spain, and France. The oil spill devastated wildlife and fisheries but also resulted in a huge response from the local population who worked tirelessly on the clean-up.

Faro de Touriñán

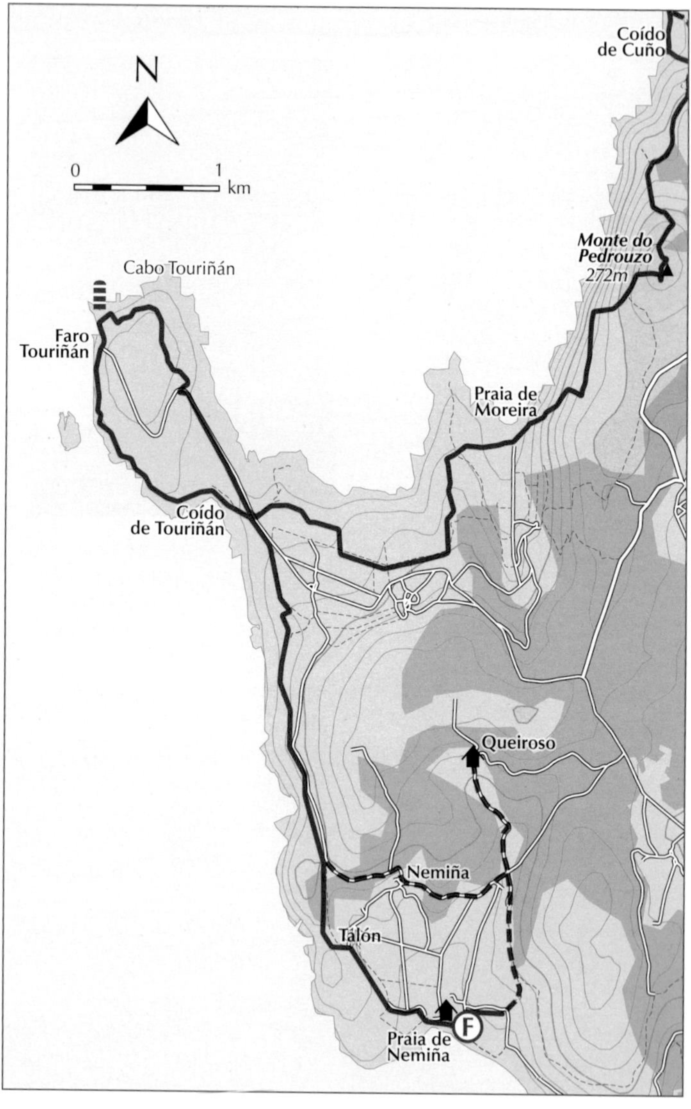
N
0
1
km
Coído
de Cuño
Monte do
Pedrouzo
272m
Cabo Touriñán
Faro
Touriñán
Praia de
Moreira
Coído
de Touriñán
Queiroso
Nemiña
Tálon
F
Praia de
Nemiña

*Faro de Touriñán*

Touriñán is the most westerly point on the Camiño dos Faros and for one month each year, 22 March to 25 April, has the last sunset on mainland Europe.

From the junction, turn right and follow a road for nearly 1km, then leave it to join a path on the right. Continue north to the headland and around it to the lighthouse, **Faro Touriñán**. The exact route is a little obscure on the ground, but keep the sea on the right and you can't go far wrong. The path on the western side of the peninsula is much easier to follow.

Go south past the lighthouse and join a cliff-top path on the other side of car park. It's a lovely path and once again we get to see the huge swell as the waves roll over the rocks. Go down to a junction almost opposite the end of offshore island, the Illa Herboso. Continue south, sticking with the coast and follow the path into a bay, the **Coído de Touriñán**, past a slipway and back up to the junction with the road to Touriñán.

Continue up the hill on the main road for about 200m, then bear right onto a wide track. After about 500m turn right onto a smaller, older track running through mostly abandoned fields. Continue south, crossing paths, onto a track through gorse, bracken and bramble that emerges, after another 600m, on a road. It's interesting landscape with farming right on the edge of viability, fighting an apparently losing battle with gorse. Continue on the road to the top of the hill and a junction with a dirt track. If you're staying in Queiroso follow the road east through Nemiña, reaching a junction after 700m. Turn left at the junction and head north. Queiroso is 800m away.

The hotel at Queiroso, the Casa Fontequeiroso (www.casafontequeiroso.com, tel +34 981 748 946) is particularly nice, more like a farm stay than a hotel.

If continuing, take a right turn onto a wide track and follow it down to a farmyard on the edge of the village of **Talón** (the dirt track turns into one made of concrete). Turn right and head south away from the village on a gravel track down towards the beach, **Praia de Nemiña**. As the track goes around pine trees, take a right-hand path down to the beach.

The Praia de Nemiña is a small surfing resort with a restaurant, surf school and a small block of apartments. The apartments get mixed reviews but there is a reservation office and I'm assured they take one-night bookings (Apartments Nemiña, tel +34 619 37 30 50).

## ALTERNATIVE SCHEDULES AND SHORTCUTS

It is possible to stay for a single night in the holiday apartments at the Praia de Nemiña, an ideal accommodation location. The alternatives at Queiroso or Lires are both excellent but a little more complicated. To get to Queiroso you need to leave the stage 2.6km from the end and walk inland for 2km (although the owner will be happy to organise a pick-up). Lires involves walking for another 90 minutes along the trail, which is a tough ask if the whole of Stage 7 has been completed.

If Stage 7 is felt to be too long, or you decide to extend it by walking to Lires, then a shortcut across any of the three peninsulas should be considered. Missing out the first or third peninsula is particularly easy.

Cutting off the trip round the Punta da Barca would mean missing a visit to the church, lighthouse and sculpture but if, for whatever reason, you made it to Muxia early on the previous day, then an early evening visit, possibly taking in the sunset, would be a good use of time. Stage 7 could then start with a trip across town joining the route on the main road west of the peninsula. This would save the best part of an hour.

The second shortcut is a little more difficult to execute and involves missing the climb around Punta da Buitra and the lovely stretch of walking along its west flank. It will, however, save about 90 minutes.

Easiest of all to execute is the third shortcut, which saves 90 minutes and chops off the tour around the Cabo Touriñán. This tour involves a complete circumnavigation with the route returning to the original departure point.

If forced to drop one peninsula, or if you haven't already visited the lighthouse in Muxia, then drop Cabo Touriñán.

# STAGE 8

*Praia de Nemiña to Cabo Fisterra*

| | |
|---|---|
| **Start** | Praia de Nemiña |
| **Finish** | Cabo Fisterra |
| **Distance** | 27km |
| **Ascent** | 820m |
| **Walking time** | 7hr 50min |

Unlike many place-to-place walks, the Camiño dos Faros finishes with a bang rather than a whimper and saves something special for the last day. On my first trip, confronted by bad weather, we got a taxi from Queiroso to Fisterra. It was a good decision as this stage includes some exposed walking. Although I've since walked this stage in less than perfect weather, the sombre grey skies didn't spoil what proved to be a lovely stretch of coastal walking and a special day.

Once the walk round the estuary, Ría de Lires, has been completed the route south is very direct. This is coastal walking at its best with spectacular cliff-top paths interspersed with big beach traverses. The final day lives up to the Camiño pledge to stay as close to the sea as possible. The cliff tops are spectacular but so are the walks across the beaches where huge enormous waves do their best to intimidate.

Technically, the walk finishes at the end of the last peninsula, upon visiting the final lighthouse at Cabo Fisterra. It's a bit of a honeypot however, not least because it's a terminal point for many pelegrinos. It's also worth remembering that somehow you have to get back to Fisterra, which is a further 2.5km down the road.

There is nowhere on the route but if you're staying in Praia de Nemiña or Queiroso, you could stop for a second breakfast at Lires.

From the apartments at the **Praia de Nemiña**, turn left onto a road and then right after 100m. Continue east to a junction with a road. The direct route from Queiroso emerges onto the main route at this point. From the junction, turn right and back to the coast following a road (for a time a track) east into the estuary. Continue along the road, which goes north over a hill, leaving the road as it descends turning right onto grassy track. Due to forestry work, this track may

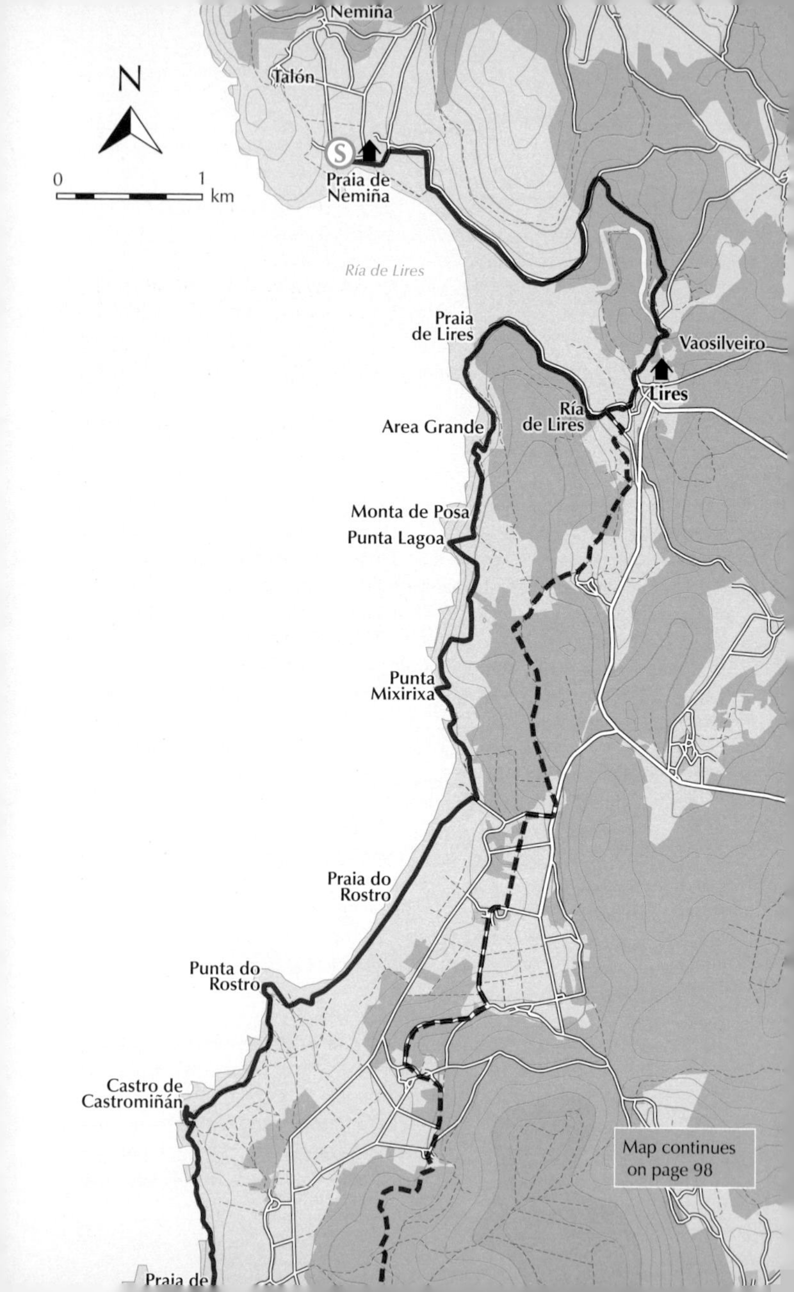
Nemiña
Talón
N
0
1
km
S
Praia de Nemiña
Ría de Lires
Praia de Lires
Vaosilveiro
Lires
Ría de Lires
Area Grande
Monta de Posa
Punta Lagoa
Punta Mixirixa
Praia do Rostro
Punta do Rostro
Castro de Castromiñán
Map continues on page 98
Praia de

be difficult to spot but follow it south for 600m contouring around valley and eventually turning right at a junction with the Camiño. Now on the Camiño, head downhill on a dirt track past a farmstead (**Vaosilveiro**). Follow a paved track over a bridge and up a hill. Using the Camiño signs to get through the village, turn left and right after 100m, heading down through **Lires** to a bridge at the head of the estuary (Ría de Lires). Here, our route parts company with the Camiño.

The river's progress to the sea is partly blocked by a sand spit near its mouth, behind which is a near lagoon. At certain times of the year the river is full of fish gorging themselves on nutrient-rich water, and the shore is dense with herons presumably enjoying rich pickings among the fish. From the bridge, follow the road along the southern shore of the estuary all the way to the narrow opening in the sand bar. At the end of road bear left round the head of a beach, **Praia de Lires**, onto a climbing dirt track.

Continue on this track all the way to the head of two linked coves, the Area Pequena and the Area Grande, and take the right-hand fork down past rocks to a path. Continue on a well-defined but potentially overgrown path round to the cliffs on the other side of the cove (**Area Grande**). Turn sharp left up a hill (ignoring a path that continues along the edge of the cliff) into pine trees. Take a right-hand fork (easily missed) and continue uphill on a track through gorse. Continue on the track as it levels out (**Monta de Posa**), turning right onto a path going southwest towards the headland, the **Punta Lagoa**.

The path around the headland is a little exposed, and on one of my trips, the fire-damaged route was marked with cairns. If the weather is bad, this stretch should be avoided. Finding the right way off the headland is important and if you're not certain of the route, go back.

When you reach the headland, head east along its southern flank on a path that starts to climb after a few metres. Go up to wall and follow a path as it turns south into trees. Watch out for peregrine falcons perching on the cliff top. Continue with a generally well-defined path across open ground, over the ridge. As the path approaches pine trees, on a descent, make a sharp turn right and follow an increasingly steep path downhill. At another dramatic location above the **Punta Mixirica**, turn left at the junction with another path and go south parallel with the sea. Follow this level path for 200m, along what are known as the cliffs of Mexadoira, emerging onto a grassy track, only to leave it and turn right after 100m. After climbing over a little wall, turn left and follow another coast-hugging path south. After crossing a stream, climb up over the ridge along a gravel track. As the gravel track heads inland, turn right towards a huge beach (**Praia do Rostro**).

Cross the beach and enjoy the spectacle of huge rollers and possibly a few surfers. Climb up rocks on the other side and take a grassy path across a gully and up to the **Punta do Rostro**. After visiting the headland and enjoying some wonderful new

views south, follow the path inland to a track and head south. Take a right fork after 200m and continue, just inland from the cliff tops, south-southwest, for 800m to where a sharp right turn takes you around the **Castro de Castromiñán**.

## THE CASON

The sinking of the Cason in December 1987 provided a pre-Prestige example of what can go wrong with a ship carrying a dangerous cargo. In this case, a storm resulted in a fire and explosion on the 9,000-ton ship, and efforts at rescue saved just eight members of the 31-man crew. One of the dead was the captain, and he was only one who knew the precise mix of chemicals in the ship's 1100-ton cargo.

The ship finally grounded on rocks near the Punta do Rostra, near the fabulous beach with the same name, and with a great hole in the bottom. Refloating the ship was not an option. Given the risk of further explosions, tugs and other boats were told to keep clear. Specialist cranes were then assembled on floating platforms and some cargo removal started. However, the weather worsened, cargo removal had to be abandoned, and some of the chemicals once again caught fire. With explosions ripping through the ship, locals started to leave, an exodus that turned into a panic as a cloud of gas emerged from the ship. Although it was subsequently reported that the cloud was not toxic, rumours were rife (speculation was that the cargo included nuclear materials) and between 15,000 and 20,000 people fled the area.

The cargo (what hadn't spilt into the sea) was removed a few days later, although given the widespread suspicion, getting rid of it proved a problem

and when workers at the Alúmina-Aluminio plant in San Cibrao were asked to deal with it, it caused a strike. The cargo was eventually returned to Antwerp, which is where most of it had come from.

After the visit to the Castro, the path returns to the track and continues its journey south, contouring along the cliffs of Gavioteiro and Arnela. Approaching the beach, **Praia de Arnela**, the path emerges onto a grassy track and heads inland, turns right onto a road and then right again onto a wide grassy path heading straight back to the cliffs. For once, the route gets round a beach without losing height.

*Rollers crashing onto the Praia da Arnela*

Turning south, the delightful, high-level contouring path continues. Waves crash noisily below and it's hard to understand how the **Punta Longa**, which as its name suggests juts right out into the sea, survives the constant battering. After 1km, the path turns sharply inland and climbs a suddenly narrow and scratchy path to a grassy track, turns right, and climbs up to the towers and equipment on top of **Monte Veladoiro** (234m). Turn right and pass between the tower and a fence to join a road. Start a long descent back down to the coast.

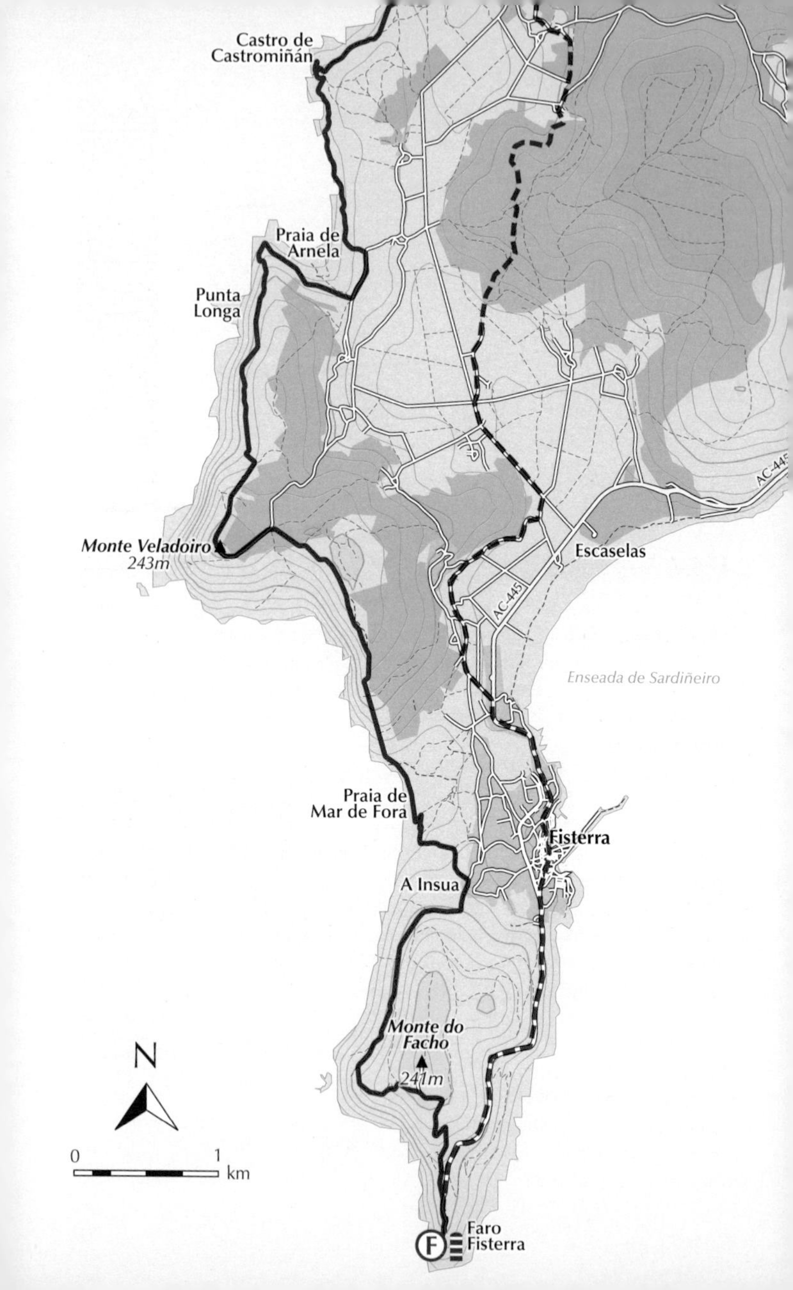

Castro de Castromiñán
Praia de Arnela
Punta Longa
Monte Veladoiro
243m
AC-445
Escaselas
AC-445
Enseada de Sardiñeiro
Praia de Mar de Fora
Fisterra
A Insua
Monte do Facho
241m
N
0
1
km
F
Faro Fisterra

*Sunset at the Praia de Mar de Afora*

## 2ND SPANISH ARMADA

Less well known than the Armada of 1588, the 2nd Spanish Armada of 1596 was even less successful. Provoked by English raids along the Atlantic coast and the spectacular sacking of Cadiz earlier in the year, Philip II made another attempt to invade England/Ireland. Almost as big as the first, the Armada came to grief in a November storm off the coast of Fisterra. 5,000 men died from either the storm or disease. A total of 38 ships were lost and the Spanish crown was bankrupted.

After about 500m turn right onto a track and right again shortly after onto another track that turns into a path as it swings across open ground. Briefly we see across what is now a peninsula, with sea to the east as well as the west. After 1km, start a steady descent that finishes at the beach (**Praia de Mar de Fora**).

Walk around two-thirds of the way across the beach, a beach whose steep drop and huge waves make it dangerous for swimming. Turn inland to some duckboards and follow them zigzagging up the hillside to the south. The duckboards are soon replaced with cobbles. Around 400m from the beach the path splits, with the left turn heading direct into Fisterra. Take this to miss out the walk to Cabo Fisterra. Otherwise, turn right and continue to into the village of **A Insua**. Turn right at a building decorated with a Camiño elf and left onto a path some 30m later.

The path (the Camiño da Insua) is particularly lovely; it has huge cobbles and is very deep, giving the impression that it has experienced centuries of heavy traffic.

## THE LOSS OF HMS CAPTAIN

The loss of HMS Captain in 1870, just off Fisterra, has the dubious honour of causing the biggest single loss of life on the Costa da Morte, with 482 deaths. The ship was the world's first ocean-going ship equipped with turreted guns (enabling the gun to swing round and shoot in different directions) but it turned out to be less stable than anticipated: in a storm off the coast of Finisterre the ship capsized, and only 27 of those on board survived.

After gaining some altitude, the path turns into a grassy track and divides twice. Take the right-hand fork each time and follow a level route above the sea. Ahead, you will see the little island of O Centelo de Fisterra. Continue on this track for 1km to a fork, turn left and start the final climb of the Camiño dos Faros, a nasty little sting in the tail, almost to the top of **Monte de Facho** (241m). Just before the top, turn right onto another track and then right again onto a road. The lighthouse, **Faro Fisterra**, should now be visible and at last we can descend although the road switches back before we make the final approach. With one little final act of defiance, our route leaves the road and climbs over rocks before conforming and, joining with everyone else, heads towards the lighthouse. The quickest way back to **Fisterra** is to follow the road.

## CABO FISTERRA

The Cabo Fisterra (Finisterra in Spanish) is the classic extension to the St James Way (Camino Francés) and visitors to Faro Fisterra, the lighthouse at the end of the peninsula, are a mix of tourists going to Spain's Land's End and pilgrims. Tranos completing the Camiño dos Faros will be in a small minority. After days of relative solitude, arriving at Europe's most visited lighthouse will provoke mixed emotions. My recommendation is not to participate in the unsavoury pellegrino tradition of burning your boots, but keep them for another trip along the Camiño dos Faros.

The Cabo Fisterra, as well as the destination for pilgrims, was a significant place in the pre-Christian era where Celts engaged in sun-worship, and from where Pheonicians set sail for Britain. It was also where couples struggling to conceive were guaranteed success (providing they perform the act on a particular local stone).

Its position en route to the Mediterranean also made in an important location for naval battles and four were fought here: Portugal versus France in 1509; Britain versus France/Spain in 1747 (twice); and Britain versus France/Spain in 1805.

*Cabo Fisterra*

The last lighthouse on the route, Faro Fisterra, was built in 1853 and its light, located 138m above sea level, can be seen from 30 miles away. Next to the lighthouse is a siren (built in 1889), which sounds on foggy days. The low-pitched sound can be heard for 20 miles and is known as the 'Vaca de Fisterra' – the cow of Fisterra. The original residents' accommodation has been converted into a hotel, although staying there is not recommended when visibility is poor!

## FISTERRA

Most 'tranos' will have a night in Fisterra before catching the bus back to Santiago de Compostela the next day. The town is located on the eastern side of the peninsula and enjoys a sheltered location. It's a pleasant place to celebrate the completion of the walk and has a good selection of bars and restaurants and, if you haven't done enough walking, it's a nice place to explore on foot.

Accommodation is plentiful but consider the Rural Prado da Viña (www.pradodavina.es, tel +34 981 740 326); the Hotel do Banco Azul (www.hoteldobancoazul.com, tel +34 981 712 391); the Mirador Fin da Terra (tel +34 981 71 23 91); and the Hotel Áncora (www.hotelancorafinisterre.com, tel +34 981 74 07 91). The bus station is in the middle of the old town and Monbus (www.monbus.es) runs at least five buses to Santiago de Compostela each day. The journey takes just under four hours.

*Approaching Praia de Arnela*

## ALTERNATIVE SCHEDULES AND SHORTCUTS

If the weather is bad, raining heavily or very windy, then alternatives should be considered. Apart from getting a taxi, the obvious other way of walking to Fisterra is to follow the Camino de Santiago variant, which has come inland from Muxia. The route can be picked up just before Lires; it heads south away from the coast before dropping down to Fisterra. Waymarking will be excellent and, without the distraction of amazing views, it should be quicker.

If you've spent the previous night in Lires, Stage 8 is easy. Otherwise, a walk all the way from Praia de Nemiña or Queiroso to Fisterra via Cabo Fisterra presents another challenging day.

If staying at Queiroso, either ask for a lift back to the route or consider walking directly down the road to rejoin the route just above Praia de Nemiña. Compared with the alternative, returning to the Camiño via Nemiña, this shortcut will save 2km.

If the tide is out, it is apparently possible to paddle across the estuary near the Praia de Nemiña, thus avoiding the walk to and from Lires and saving 1hr 50min. Check tide times and ask advice locally before taking to the water, and make sure your phone isn't in your pocket.

Depending on your Fisterra departure plans, consider visiting the Cabo Fisterra and completing the Camiño the next day. Once the last beach, Praia do Mar de Fóra, has been crossed, it's a short walk into Fisterra from the west.

# APPENDIX A

*Trek planning table*

| | Hotel | Restaurant | Cumulative distance | Cumulative Time | Shortcut | Page |
|---|---|---|---|---|---|---|
| **Stage 1** | | | | | | **28** |
| Porto de Malpica | Y | Y | – | – | | |
| Praia de Area Maior | | | 1km | 15min | | |
| Ermida de San Adrián | | | 4km | 1hr | | |
| Praia de Beo | | | 8.5km | 2hr 10min | | |
| Restaurante Seiruga | | Y | 11km | 2hr 45min | | |
| Hostal Casa da Vasca | Y | Y | 13km | 3hr 15min | | |
| Bar Xan | | Y | 13.5km | 3hr 25min | | |
| Faro de Punta Nariga | | | 18.5km | 5hr | | |
| Praia de Niñóns | | | 22km | 6hr | | |
| **Stage 2** | | | | | | **38** |
| Praia de Niñóns | | | – | – | | |
| Porto de Santa Mariña | | | 2km | 35min | | |
| Punta Espiñeira | | | 6km | 2hr | | |
| Roncudo | | | 9km | 3hr | Head south to O Porte de Corme – save 1hr | |

| | Hotel | Restaurant | Cumulative distance | Cumulative Time | Shortcut | Page |
|---|---|---|---|---|---|---|
| Faro do Roncudo | | | 12.5km | 4hr 10min | | |
| O Porte de Corme | Y | Y | 15.5km | 5hr | | |
| Praia de Valarés | | | 20.5km | 6hr 30min | | |
| Ponte de Ponteceso | Y | Y | 26km | 7hr 45min | | |
| **Stage 3** | | | | | | **48** |
| Ponte de Ponteceso | | | – | – | | |
| Start of Rego dos Muiños | | Y | 7km | 1hr 45min | Miss out inland trip and save 1hr 50min | |
| Castro de Borneiro | | | 10.5km | 2hr 40min | | |
| Vilaseco | | | 11km | 2hr 55min | | |
| Dólmen de Dombate | | | 12.5km | 3hr 15min | | |
| Fontefría | | | 14km | 3hr 40min | | |
| Castelo de Lourido | | | 15km | 4hr 5min | | |
| Arnela | | | 16.5km | 4hr 20min | | |
| Canduas | | | 17km | 4hr 30min | | |
| Punta Rubia | | | 22km | 6hr | | |
| Praia de Laxe | | | 23.5km | 6hr 15min | | |
| Laxe | Y | Y | 25km | 6hr 35min | | |

| | | | | | | |
|---|---|---|---|---|---|---|
| **Stage 4** | | | | | | **58** |
| Laxe | | | – | – | | |
| Faro de Laxe | | | 2km | 30min | | |
| Peñón de Soesto | | | 4km | 1hr 45min | | |
| Praia de Soesto | | | 4.5km | 2hr | | |
| Punta Catasol | | | 6km | 2hr 30min | | |
| Praia de Traba | | | 8.5km | 3hr 10min | | |
| Bar O Mórdomo | | Y | 11km | 3hr 45min | | |
| Camelle | | Y | 15.5km | 5hr 15min | | |
| German Hermit's House | | | 15.5km | 5hr 20min | | |
| Arou | | Y | 18km | 5hr 55min | | |
| **Stage 5** | | | | | | **65** |
| Arou | | | – | – | | |
| Porto de Santa Mariña | | | 4km | 1hr 15min | | |
| Coído de Santa Mariña | | | 4.5km | 1hr 35min | | |
| Duna de Monte Branco | | | 5.5km | 2hr 15min | | |
| Cementerio dos Ingleses | | | 8km | 3hr | | |
| Punta do Boi | | | 8.5km | 3hr 15min | | |
| Faro Vilán | | Y | 15km | 5hr 15min | Miss visit to lighthouse, save 1hr | |

| | Hotel | Restaurant | Cumulative distance | Cumulative Time | Shortcut | Page |
|---|---|---|---|---|---|---|
| Ermita de Nosa Señora do Montea | | | 19km | 6hr 30min | Miss visit to the Ermita de Nosa Señora do Montea, save 40min | |
| Porto de Camariñas | Y | Y | 23km | 7hr 40min | | |
| **Stage 6** | | | | | | 75 |
| Porto de Camariñas | | | – | – | | |
| Praia de Lingunde | | | 2km | 35min | | |
| O Cruceiro | | | 5km | 1hr 20min | Continue on main road to O Ariño, save 1hr | |
| Restuarant – O Ariño | | Y | 9.5km | 2hr 35min | | |
| Tasaraño | | | 9.5km | 2hr 40min | | |
| Dor | | | 11km | 3hr | | |
| O Allo | | | 12km | 3hr 20min | | |
| Ponte do Porto | Y | Y | 13km | 3hr 45min | | |
| Cereixo | | | 14.5km | 4hr 15min | | |
| Faro Playa do Lago | | | 20.5km | 6hr | | |
| Playa de Lago | Y | Y | 21km | 6hr 10min | | |
| Merexo | | | 22.5km | 6hr 35min | | |
| Os Muiños | | | 24.5km | 7hr 10min | | |

| | | | | | | |
|---|---|---|---|---|---|---|
| Praia de Merexo | | | 25.5km | 7hr 30min | | |
| Chorente | | | 27km | 7hr 55min | | |
| Muxía | Y | Y | 29.5km | 8hr 40min | | |
| **Stage 7** | | | | | | **84** |
| Muxía | | | - | – | | |
| Faro de Muxia | | | 1km | 20min | | |
| Santuario Nosa Señora da Barca | | | 1km | 25min | Cut across peninsula and save 50min | |
| Praia de Lourido | | | 4km | 1hr 10min | | |
| Punta de Lourido | | | 5km | 1hr 30min | | |
| Monte Cachelmo | | | 6km | 1hr 50min | | |
| Monte Buitra | | | 9.5km | 2hr 50min | Miss Monte Buitra and save 1hr 30min | |
| Monte do Pedrouzo | | | 13.5km | 4hr 5min | | |
| Faro Touriñán | | | 20.5km | 5hr 55min | Miss Faro Touriñán and save 1hr 30min | |
| Coído de Touriñán | | | 22.5km | 6hr 20min | | |
| Turn-off to Hotel | Y | | 25km | 7hr | Add 30min if walking to hotel | |
| Talón | | | 26km | 7hr 10min | | |
| Praia de Nemiña | | Y | 26.5km | 7hr 25min | | |

| | Hotel | Restaurant | Cumulative distance | Cumulative Time | Shortcut | Page |
|---|---|---|---|---|---|---|
| **Stage 8** | | | | | | 93 |
| Praia de Nemiña | | | – | – | | |
| Lires | Y | Y | 5.5km | 1hr 35min | | |
| Praia de Lires | | | 7.5km | 2hr | If tide is out, consider crossing direct to Praia de Lires to save 1hr 50min | |
| Praia do Rostro | | | 11.5km | 3hr 15min | | |
| Castro de Castromiñán | | | 15km | 4hr 20min | | |
| Praia de Arnela | | | 17km | 5hr | | |
| Veladoiro | | | 20km | 5hr 50min | | |
| Praia de Mar de Fora | | | 22.5km | 6hr 30min | Could head directly into Fisterra here | |
| A Insua | | Y | 23.5km | 6hr 50min | | |
| Monte Facho | | | 26km | 7hr 30min | | |
| Faro Fisterra | Y | Y | 27km | 7hr 50min | | |

# APPENDIX B

*Accommodation*

## Stage 1

### Porto de Malpica

Hotel Fonte de Fraile (located to the west of the town centre)
www.hotelfontedofraile.com
tel +34 981 720 732

Pensión Penchito (town centre location)
www.pensionpanchito.com
tel +34 981 720 307

Hostal Malpica
tel +34 981 72 19 06

### As Garzas

Pensión Rústica Casa da Vasca
www.casadavasca.com
tel +34 981 721 960

As Garzas (Michelin star)
www.asgarzas.com
tel +34 981 720 605

## Stage 2

### Porte de Corme

Apartamentos Turísticos Playa de Osmo
www.playadeosmo.com
tel +34 981 705 278

### Ponteceso

Pensión Teyma
www.pensionteyma.com
tel +34 981 715 404

## Stage 3

### Laxe

Hostal Bahía
www.bahialaxe.com
tel +34 981 728 207

Hostal Playa de Laxe
www.playadelaxe.com
tel +34 981 739 000

Caso do Arco
www.casadoarco.es
tel +34 981 706 904

## Stage 4

Return to Laxe or go on to Camariñas.

## Stage 5

### Camariñas

Hotel Puerto Arnela (best location)
www.hotelpuertoarnela.com
tel +34 981 737 240

Hotel O Paranda
www.oparranda.com
tel +34 677 433 303

Pensión Gaviota
tel +34 981 736 326

Stella del Mar (located away from seafront)
tel +34 981 737 304

**Ponte do Porto**

Hostal O Pincho
tel +34 981 730 250

**Praia do Lago**

Hostal Praia do Lago (summer months only) www.hotelplayadelago.com
tel +34 981 750 793

**Stage 6**

**Muxia**

Hotel de Encanto A de Loló
www.hoteladelolo.com
tel +34 981 742 422

Hostal de la Cruz
www.hostallacruz.com
tel +34 981 742 084

Hábitat Cm Muxia
tel +34 981 742 148

The Parador Muxia above the Praia de Lourido will presumably be taking bookings at some point from 2020 onwards.

Pilgrim accommodation also available.

**Stage 7**

**Queiroso**

Casa Fontequeiroso
www.casafontequeiroso.com
tel +34 981 748 946

**Praia de Nemiña**

Apartments Nemiña
tel +34 619 37 3050

**Lires**

As Eiras Lires
www.ruralaseiras.com
tel +34 981 748 180

Casa Lourido
www.casalourido.es
tel +34 981 74 82 03

**Stage 8**

**Cabo Fisterra**

O Semafaro (hotel next to the lighthouse)
www.hotelsemaforodefisterra.com
tel +34 607 778 240

**Fisterra**

A big choice of hotels including:

Hotel Rural Prado da Viña
www.pradodavina.es
tel +34 981 740 326

Hotel do Banco Azul
www.hoteldobancoazul.com
tel +34 981 712 391

Mirador Fin da Terra
tel +34 981 71 23 91

Hotel Áncora
www.hotelancorafinisterre.com
tel +34 981 74 07 91

# APPENDIX C

*Main Galician festivals*

| Location | Festival | Date |
|---|---|---|
| Fisterra | Festa do Santo Cristo | Holy week |
| Corme | Festa do Percebe | First Saturday in July |
| Carnés | La Faguía de Carnés | 9 July |
| Corme | Festa da Virxe do Carme | 16 July |
| Malpica | Festa de San Adrián | Second weekend in July |
| Camariñas | Festa da Virxe do Carme | 16 July |
| Fisterra | Festa do Longueirón and Encontro Pirata | First weekend of August |
| Cabana | Pilgrimage of San Fins do Castro | First weekend of August |
| Malpica | Festa Galega | Mid August |
| Malpica | Festas do Mar | Fourth week in August |
| Laxe | Festas de Laxe | 14 and 17 August |
| Corme | Festa de San Roque | Last weekend in August |
| Muxia | Mercedes Rutas do Mar | Various days in August |
| Muxia | Festas da Barca | Second week of September |
| Pontesco | Festas das Barquiñas | Second week of September |
| Corme | Festas da Virxe dos Remedios | End of September |
| Pontesco | Feira das Fabas | Last Saturday in October |

# APPENDIX D

*Useful contacts*

**Camiño dos Faros**

Association O Camiño dos Faros
www.caminodosfaros.com
traskimail@gmail.comFacebook:
Caminodosfaros and Traskicostadamorte

**Public transport**

Transporte Público de Galicia
www.bus.gal/gl

Arriva
www.arriva.gal

Monbus
www.monbus.es/es/galicia/rutas-regionales

RENFE
www.renfe.com

When planning your travel, consider using the excellent Rome-to-Rio website, which picks up website information from all the main travel operators (www.Rome2Rio.com).

# NOTES

# NOTES

## DOWNLOAD THE ROUTES IN GPX FORMAT

All the routes in this guide are available for download from:

**www.cicerone.co.uk/971/GPX**

as GPX files. You should be able to load them into most formats of mobile device, whether GPS or smartphone.

When you go to this link, you will be asked for your email address and where you purchased the guide, and have the option to subscribe to the Cicerone e-newsletter.

CICERONE

www.cicerone.co.uk

# LISTING OF CICERONE GUIDES

**SCOTLAND**

Backpacker's Britain: Northern Scotland
Ben Nevis and Glen Coe
Cycling in the Hebrides
Great Mountain Days in Scotland
Mountain Biking in Southern and Central Scotland
Mountain Biking in West and North West Scotland
Not the West Highland Way
Scotland
Scotland's Best Small Mountains
Scotland's Mountain Ridges
Scrambles in Lochaber
The Ayrshire and Arran Coastal Paths
The Border Country
The Borders Abbeys Way
The Cape Wrath Trail
The Great Glen Way
The Great Glen Way Map Booklet
The Hebridean Way
The Hebrides
The Isle of Mull
The Isle of Skye
The Skye Trail
The Southern Upland Way
The Speyside Way
The Speyside Way Map Booklet
The West Highland Way
Walking Highland Perthshire
Walking in Scotland's Far North
Walking in the Angus Glens
Walking in the Cairngorms
Walking in the Ochils, Campsie Fells and Lomond Hills
Walking in the Pentland Hills
Walking in the Southern Uplands
Walking in Torridon
Walking Loch Lomond and the Trossachs
Walking on Arran
Walking on Harris and Lewis
Walking on Rum and the Small Isles
Walking on the Orkney and Shetland Isles
Walking on Uist and Barra
Walking the Corbetts Vol 1 South of the Great Glen
Walking the Corbetts Vol 2 North of the Great Glen
Walking the Munros Vol 1 – Southern, Central and Western Highlands
Walking the Munros Vol 2 – Northern Highlands and the Cairngorms
West Highland Way Map Booklet
Winter Climbs Ben Nevis and Glen Coe
Winter Climbs in the Cairngorms

**NORTHERN ENGLAND TRAILS**

Hadrian's Wall Path
Hadrian's Wall Path Map Booklet
Pennine Way Map Booklet
The Coast to Coast Map Booklet
The Coast to Coast Walk
The Dales Way
The Dales Way Map Booklet
The Pennine Way

**LAKE DISTRICT**

Cycling in the Lake District
Great Mountain Days in the Lake District
Lake District Winter Climbs
Lake District: High Level and Fell Walks
Lake District: Low Level and Lake Walks
Mountain Biking in the Lake District
Outdoor Adventures with Children – Lake District
Scrambles in the Lake District – North
Scrambles in the Lake District – South
Short Walks in Lakeland Book 1: South Lakeland
Short Walks in Lakeland Book 2: North Lakeland
Short Walks in Lakeland Book 3: West Lakeland
The Cumbria Way
Tour of the Lake District
Trail and Fell Running in the Lake District

**NORTH WEST ENGLAND AND THE ISLE OF MAN**

Cycling the Pennine Bridleway
Cycling the Way of the Roses
Isle of Man Coastal Path
The Lancashire Cycleway
The Lune Valley and Howgills
The Ribble Way
Walking in Cumbria's Eden Valley
Walking in Lancashire
Walking in the Forest of Bowland and Pendle
Walking on the Isle of Man
Walking on the West Pennine Moors
Walks in Ribble Country
Walks in Silverdale and Arnside

**NORTH EAST ENGLAND, YORKSHIRE DALES AND PENNINES**

Cycling in the Yorkshire Dales
Great Mountain Days in the Pennines
Mountain Biking in the Yorkshire Dales
South Pennine Walks
St Oswald's Way and St Cuthbert's Way
The Cleveland Way and the Yorkshire Wolds Way
The Cleveland Way Map Booklet
The North York Moors
The Reivers Way
The Teesdale Way
Trail and Fell Running in the Yorkshire Dales
Walking in County Durham
Walking in Northumberland
Walking in the North Pennines
Walking in the Yorkshire Dales: North and East
Walking in the Yorkshire Dales: South and West
Walks in Dales Country
Walks in the Yorkshire Dales

**WALES AND WELSH BORDERS**

Cycling Lôn Las Cymru
Glyndwr's Way
Great Mountain Days in Snowdonia
Hillwalking in Shropshire
Hillwalking in Wales – Vol 1
Hillwalking in Wales – Vol 2
Mountain Walking in Snowdonia
Offa's Dyke Map Booklet
Offa's Dyke Path
Ridges of Snowdonia
Scrambles in Snowdonia
The Ascent of Snowdon
The Ceredigion and Snowdonia Coast Paths
The Pembrokeshire Coast Path
Pembrokeshire Coast Path Map Booklet
The Severn Way
The Snowdonia Way
The Wales Coast Path
The Wye Valley Walk
Walking in Carmarthenshire
Walking in Pembrokeshire
Walking in the Forest of Dean
Walking in the South Wales Valleys
Walking in the Wye Valley
Walking on the Brecon Beacons
Walking on the Gower

### DERBYSHIRE, PEAK DISTRICT AND MIDLANDS

Cycling in the Peak District
Dark Peak Walks
Scrambles in the Dark Peak
Walking in Derbyshire
White Peak Walks: The Northern Dales
White Peak Walks: The Southern Dales

### SOUTHERN ENGLAND

20 Classic Sportive Rides in South East England
20 Classic Sportive Rides in South West England
Cycling in the Cotswolds
Mountain Biking on the North Downs
Mountain Biking on the South Downs
North Downs Way Map Booklet
South West Coast Path Map Booklet – Vol 1: Minehead to St Ives
South West Coast Path Map Booklet – Vol 2: St Ives to Plymouth
South West Coast Path Map Booklet – Vol 3: Plymouth to Poole
Suffolk Coast and Heath Walks
The Cotswold Way
The Cotswold Way Map Booklet
The Great Stones Way
The Kennet and Avon Canal
The Lea Valley Walk
The North Downs Way
The Peddars Way and Norfolk Coast path
The Pilgrims' Way
The Ridgeway Map Booklet
The Ridgeway National Trail
The South Downs Way
The South Downs Way Map Booklet
The South West Coast Path
The Thames Path
The Thames Path Map Booklet
The Two Moors Way
Two Moors Way Map Booklet
Walking Hampshire's Test Way
Walking in Cornwall
Walking in Essex
Walking in Kent
Walking in London
Walking in Norfolk
Walking in Sussex
Walking in the Chilterns
Walking in the Cotswolds
Walking in the Isles of Scilly
Walking in the New Forest
Walking in the North Wessex Downs
Walking in the Thames Valley
Walking on Dartmoor
Walking on Guernsey
Walking on Jersey
Walking on the Isle of Wight
Walking the Jurassic Coast
Walks in the South Downs National Park

### BRITISH ISLES CHALLENGES, COLLECTIONS AND ACTIVITIES

The Book of the Bivvy
The Book of the Bothy
The C2C Cycle Route
The End to End Cycle Route
The Mountains of England and Wales: Vol 1 Wales
The Mountains of England and Wales: Vol 2 England
The National Trails
The UK's County Tops
Three Peaks, Ten Tors

### ALPS CROSS-BORDER ROUTES

100 Hut Walks in the Alps
Across the Eastern Alps: E5
Alpine Ski Mountaineering Vol 1 – Western Alps
Alpine Ski Mountaineering Vol 2 – Central and Eastern Alps
Chamonix to Zermatt
The Karnischer Hohenweg
The Tour of the Bernina
Tour of Mont Blanc
Tour of Monte Rosa
Tour of the Matterhorn
Trail Running – Chamonix and the Mont Blanc region
Trekking in the Alps
Trekking in the Silvretta and Rätikon Alps
Trekking Munich to Venice
Walking in the Alps

### PYRENEES AND FRANCE/SPAIN CROSS-BORDER ROUTES

The GR10 Trail
The GR11 Trail
The Pyrenean Haute Route
The Pyrenees
The Way of St James – Spain
Walks and Climbs in the Pyrenees

### AUSTRIA

Innsbruck Mountain Adventures
The Adlerweg
Trekking in Austria's Hohe Tauern
Trekking in the Stubai Alps
Trekking in the Zillertal Alps
Walking in Austria

### SWITZERLAND

Cycle Touring in Switzerland
Switzerland's Jura Crest Trail
The Swiss Alpine Pass Route – Via Alpina Route 1
The Swiss Alps
Tour of the Jungfrau Region
Walking in the Bernese Oberland
Walking in the Valais

### FRANCE AND BELGIUM

Chamonix Mountain Adventures
Cycle Touring in France
Cycling London to Paris
Cycling the Canal de la Garonne
Cycling the Canal du Midi
Écrins National Park
Mont Blanc Walks
Mountain Adventures in the Maurienne
The GR20 Corsica
The GR5 Trail
The GR5 Trail – Vosges and Jura
The Grand Traverse of the Massif Central
The Loire Cycle Route
The Moselle Cycle Route
The River Rhone Cycle Route
The Robert Louis Stevenson Trail
The Way of St James – Le Puy to the Pyrenees
Tour of the Oisans: The GR54
Tour of the Queyras
Vanoise Ski Touring
Via Ferratas of the French Alps
Walking in Corsica
Walking in Provence – East
Walking in Provence – West
Walking in the Auvergne
Walking in the Briançonnais
Walking in the Cevennes
Walking in the Dordogne
Walking in the Haute Savoie: North
Walking in the Haute Savoie: South
Walks in the Cathar Region
The GR5 Trail – Benelux and Lorraine
Walking in the Ardennes

### GERMANY

Hiking and Cycling in the Black Forest
The Danube Cycleway Vol 1
The Rhine Cycle Route
The Westweg
Walking in the Bavarian Alps

### ICELAND AND GREENLAND

Trekking in Greenland – The Arctic Circle Trail
Walking and Trekking in Iceland

## IRELAND

The Irish Coast to Coast Walk
The Mountains of Ireland
The Wild Atlantic Way and Western Ireland

## ITALY

Italy's Sibillini National Park
Shorter Walks in the Dolomites
Ski Touring and Snowshoeing in the Dolomites
The Way of St Francis
Through the Italian Alps
Trekking in the Apennines
Trekking in the Dolomites
Via Ferratas of the Italian Dolomites: Vol 1
Via Ferratas of the Italian Dolomites: Vol 2
Walking and Trekking in the Gran Paradiso
Walking in Abruzzo
Walking in Italy's Stelvio National Park
Walking in Sardinia
Walking in Sicily
Walking in the Dolomites
Walking in Tuscany
Walking in Umbria
Walking Lake Garda and Iseo
Walking on the Amalfi Coast
Walking the Italian Lakes
Walks and Treks in the Maritime Alps

## SCANDINAVIA

Walking in Norway

## EASTERN EUROPE AND THE BALKANS

The Danube Cycleway Vol 2
The High Tatras
The Mountains of Romania
Walking in Bulgaria's National Parks
Walking in Hungary
Mountain Biking in Slovenia
The Islands of Croatia
The Julian Alps of Slovenia
The Mountains of Montenegro
The Peaks of the Balkans Trail
The Slovenian Mountain Trail
Walking in Croatia
Walking in Slovenia: The Karavanke

## SPAIN AND PORTUGAL

Coastal Walks in Andalucia
Cycle Touring in Spain
Cycling the Camino de Santiago
Mountain Walking in Mallorca
Mountain Walking in Southern Catalunya
Spain's Sendero Histórico: The GR1
The Andalucian Coast to Coast Walk
The Mountains of Nerja
The Mountains of Ronda and Grazalema
The Northern Caminos
The Sierras of Extremadura
Trekking in Mallorca
Walking and Trekking in the Sierra Nevada
Walking in Andalucia
Walking in Menorca
Walking in the Cordillera Cantabrica
Walking on Gran Canaria
Walking on La Gomera and El Hierro
Walking on La Palma
Walking on Lanzarote and Fuerteventura
Walking on Tenerife
Walking on the Costa Blanca
The Camino Portugués
Walking in Portugal
Walking in the Algarve
Walking on Madeira

## GREECE, CYPRUS AND MALTA

The High Mountains of Crete
Trekking in Greece
Walking and Trekking in Zagori
Walking and Trekking on Corfu
Walking in Cyprus
Walking on Malta

## INTERNATIONAL CHALLENGES, COLLECTIONS AND ACTIVITIES

Canyoning in the Alps
Europe's High Points
The Via Francigena Canterbury to Rome – Part 2

## AFRICA

Mountaineering in the Moroccan High Atlas
The High Atlas
Trekking in the Atlas Mountains
Walks and Scrambles in the Moroccan Anti-Atlas
Kilimanjaro
Walking in the Drakensberg

## ASIA

Trekking in Tajikistan
Japan's Kumano Kodo Pilgrimage
Walking and Trekking in the Japan Alps and Mount Fuji
Jordan – Walks, Treks, Caves, Climbs and Canyons
Treks and Climbs in Wadi Rum, Jordan
Annapurna
Everest: A Trekker's Guide
Trekking in the Himalaya
Trekking in Bhutan
Trekking in Ladakh
The Mount Kailash Trek

## NORTH AMERICA

British Columbia
The John Muir Trail
The Pacific Crest Trail

## SOUTH AMERICA

Aconcagua and the Southern Andes
Hiking and Biking Peru's Inca Trails
Torres del Paine

## TECHNIQUES

Fastpacking
Geocaching in the UK
Indoor Climbing
Lightweight Camping
Map and Compass
Outdoor Photography
Polar Exploration
Rock Climbing
Sport Climbing
The Mountain Hut Book

## MINI GUIDES

Alpine Flowers
Avalanche!
Navigation
Pocket First Aid and Wilderness Medicine
Snow

## MOUNTAIN LITERATURE

8000 metres
A Walk in the Clouds
Abode of the Gods
Fifty Years of Adventure
The Pennine Way – the Path, the People, the Journey
Unjustifiable Risk?

For full information on all our guides, books and eBooks, visit our website:
**www.cicerone.co.uk**